NEEDLE FELTING
FROM BASICS TO BEARS

with step-by-step photos and instructions
for creating cute little bears and bunnies from natural wools

Liza Adams

STACKPOLE BOOKS

0 11557 01662 8

DEDICATION

To my wonderful family and friends, who always believed in me and reminded me that it was OK to do what I love. And to my amazing customers who keep coming back for more and sharing my work around the world. Thank you all for loving what I do and supporting me while I do it!

Text and photographs © Liza Adams, 2016
Typographical design © David Bateman Ltd, 2016

Published in North America in 2016 by
STACKPOLE BOOKS
An imprint of Globe Pequot
Trade Division of The Rowman & Littlefield Publishing Group, 4501 Forbes Boulevard, Suite 200, Lanham, Maryland 20706
www.stackpolebooks.com

Distributed by NATIONAL BOOK NETWORK 800-462-6420

All rights reserved, including the right to reproduce this book or portions thereof in any form or by any means, electronic or mechanical, including recording or by any information storage and retrieval system, without permission in writing from the publisher. All inquiries should be addressed to Stackpole Books, 5067 Ritter Road, Mechanicsburg, PA 17055.

The contents of this book are for personal use only. Patterns contained herein may be reproduced in limited quantities for such use. Any large-scale commercial reproduction is prohibited without the written consent of the publisher.

Printed in China through Colorcraft Ltd, Hong Kong

10 9 8 7 6 5 4 3

First edition

Cover design by Wendy A. Reynolds

Cataloging-in-Publication Data is on file with the Library of Congress

ISBN 978-0-8117-1662-8

CONTENTS

INTRODUCTION

BEGINNER PROJECTS

INTERMEDIATE PROJECTS

ADVANCED PROJECTS

HOW TO DO MORE

ABOUT THE BOOK

Over the following pages you will learn how to work with fiber to create some wonderful pieces. As you progress through the projects, you will learn all the basics of the craft of needle felting, along with skills and techniques to create something really special.

BEGINNER PROJECTS

In the first project you learn how to create a felted ornament. This will teach you a number of things which we will work with later in the book: how to create a firm project, how to use your needles and how to cover and decorate your piece. These techniques will help you to understand how the craft works and how it can be manipulated to suit each artist so that you can create something that is uniquely you. Also in this section, you will learn how to make a cupcake pincushion and a pin to wear.

With these three projects, you are equipped to try the more complex items taught later in the book. I highly recommend you work through each project, even if you can't think of anyone you would give the finished piece to, because it will still teach you essential techniques to ensure success.

INTERMEDIATE PROJECTS

Once you know the basics, you will learn how to connect the parts of an item together. The first project in this section is the keychain, which will show you how to attach eyes and ears to your work.

The second project is a doll that has a jointed head and there are a few new techniques in this project for you to try.

These two pieces will give you a taste of the skills you need for the final project in this section—the basic jointed bear. Making the keychain and doll before you attempt the bear will be of great benefit to your needle-felting skills, so I hope you will work through the book so you get the best results.

*All projects are 3½–4 in (9–10 cm) high.

ADVANCED PROJECTS

In the last section there are just two projects: a bear and a rabbit. Taking what you have learned so far, you will add some new dimensions to your work. I would suggest that before you start on this section, you make a number of basic bears first. In this way you will have a real feel for how the bears are made and have a better understanding of the quantities of fiber needed for each piece. Learning how much fiber you need takes time and is a process of trial and error. Learning by doing is the best way.

Once you start this project, you will learn how to make the head in one piece rather than two. This is actually a more difficult technique and will teach you about sculpting and shaping. We will also be looking at getting more shape into the limbs, such as through my favorite style, the dropped paws.

The second project will teach you how to make a rabbit, as I'm sure you will want to branch out a bit after a few bears and make other critters too. This project shows how to make big, puffy cheeks, which you can use with critters other than rabbits as well. You will, of course, learn how to make nice long ears and big bunny feet as well as a little cotton tail!

HOW TO DO MORE

The last part of the book offers a gallery of shapes and ideas that will allow you to take the skills you have learned in the previous projects and create anything from cats, dogs, and mice to your own fantasy animals. There are also step-by-step photos that show you how to add details such as pointed ears, foot pads, patches and more to make your creation truly one-of-a-kind.

I hope that this book will be entertaining, informative and set you on a path of creative enjoyment. I love needle felting. I have spent the last 10 years mastering the craft and even now I am always learning something new, something I can do differently or a new trick to enjoy. Over 800 bears have helped me form my techniques, and many students have taught me how to teach. I hope that this shows as you follow my lessons, sculpt your projects and share your creations with your friends and family.

Liza Adams

Little Handfuls
MINI BEARS

*All projects are 3½–4 in (9–10 cm) high.

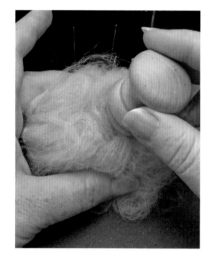

WHAT IS NEEDLE FELTING?

I always find this to be rather a big question. It is just something that I do, and after doing it for so long it has become second nature to me. I don't tend to think about how I do it. This makes the process of writing instructions a good exercise for me. But even then, I can tell you how to needle felt more easily than I can explain what it is!

There are a number of basic descriptions, and if asked at a show I will usually say: "Needle felting is taking loose fiber, mixing it all up and then poking it with special needles. These needles have unique shafts with various barbs along them. Poking these in and out of the fiber will cause it to tangle up, and as the fibers tangle they compact down and get firmer. In this way needle felters are able to sculpt the fiber into the shape they want."

I say sculpt because that is really what we are doing. Once you start working with the needles and fibers you will see what I mean. I find that when I start a piece it is very soft and has no shape or substance but as I work it there comes a point where it firms up and is able to be sculpted.

Perhaps in this way it is similar to a sculptor working with clay; you have to prepare the clay, whatever kind you are using, so that it is ready to be worked into something amazing. It is the same with the fiber. Once it is holding together, you can manipulate and sculpt with the needle to get it into the shape you need. No matter what size you like to work in the premise is the same, but remember that the more wool you use, the longer it takes!

Needle felting is a very unusual craft, unlike any other I have done. I love teaching it and hearing from my students how their friends and families react when they go home after their first lesson. Most come back the next week and say, "No one knows what I'm talking about!" Needle felting is just one of those things that makes more sense when you see it rather than hear about it. Though I will never forget the woman who came up to me at a show and, after watching for a few minutes, said: "So if I poke at some wool with a needle it will turn into a bear?" From memory my reply was to stutter and stammer my way through the above description as I was so surprised at her take on the situation. But what I really wanted to say was: "Only in the same way that if you water bare earth it will turn into a wonderful garden!"

You have to have skill, talent and knowledge to create something wonderful from nothing, and I hope to help you achieve your own wonderful creations in the following pages.

TOOLS REQUIRED

NEEDLES

I try to keep the tools as simple as possible. You need felting needles, naturally, but there are over 30 grades of needles and every country has different grading systems and sizes. This can get complicated, so in this book I work with just two needles — one larger and one smaller.

Also, needles *will* break. You may break *many* needles. Some of my students have broken two or three every lesson for the first few weeks! It just depends on your technique as you learn. Once you refine your methods, breakages are much less common.

You need to experiment for yourself, see what needles are available and how they work with the fiber you can source. Balancing the needles and the fiber is important. Your choice of needle will depend on the grade of fiber. If you can only source coarse fiber, you won't want to use very fine needles as they will take a very long time to compact your fiber down into something you can work with. What should only take you four hours will end up taking six or more. Conversely, if you can only source lovely fine merino fiber you won't want to be using very big needles as the fiber will resist the bigger needles and not felt down at all.

I didn't use merino for years, as I found it hard to work with and it took so much longer to get firm. But you have to work with what you can, so as long as you can match your needles to your fiber that will be a good start.

In the book I use a 36T, a 38T and a 40T. The 36T is the larger needle and the T stands for Triangle. There are also star-shaped and other shaped needles for specific tasks, such as making dents. I use the 40T, which is smaller, for finishing on fiber that isn't firming up or becoming smooth, usually merino. So if I work with a coarser fiber I use 36 with 38 to finish, but if I am working with merino I would use 38 with 40 to finish.

I also use a multi-needle tool for the projects. Something

Shown above are a 38T needle (left) and a 36T needle (the longer needle), alongside a close-up at right showing the barbs.

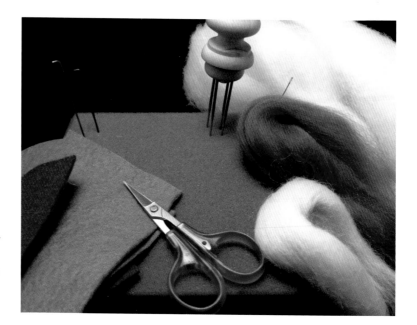

All you need for a basic needle-felting project – fiber, a couple of needle sizes, a multi-needle tool if you have one, and some good craft scissors.

similar to the one pictured above is available in most stores that sell felting needles. Multi-needle tools come in different shapes and can take different amounts of needles. This one takes four, and you can put any grade needle you like in them. I usually fill mine with 36T needles and use it to start off larger pieces like heads and bodies, or for making ornaments (see the first project), which use a lot of fiber. You can also buy pen-style needle holders, but most of the brands I've seen have been quite expensive.

You can make your own multi-needle tools using an oven-baked clay such as Fimo. I have a 2-needle tool that I made six years ago and I still use it every time I felt. Just wrap the ends of the needles in the clay, making sure there is no movement and they are both very straight, then bake according to the manufacturer's instructions.

FIBER

I work with a lot of home-dyed fibers, which means that I don't always know exactly what fiber I'm using. Where I live, in New Zealand, we are lucky to have a lot of wool available to us. I like to work with Corriedale and Romney wools and I find them especially good for beginners. Both these wools are coarser than merino top, which is super fine. But they are not too coarse so that your work still has a nice finish.

The fibers you use will depend on local availability, but you should be able to find something similar. With the Internet, of course, you can buy almost anything you like, so if you don't have much available locally get online and buy from the larger online suppliers. They should have information on their fibers and their suitability for felting.

Don't buy anything that is shrink-resistant (super wash), as this fiber is specially designed *not* to felt up when spun into yarn and then thrown in the washing machine! And, of course, we need it to felt up!

I have used merino batts, imported from the United States. You can use them in the same way as other fiber for needle felting, but they don't need to be mixed as much at the start of your work as they are already mixed.

If you are trying a new supplier or fiber, just buy a little, or see if they will send you samples (some places will, especially a local grower who is trying to increase their business). You only need 1¾ oz (50 g) bags to make up to four bears so a little fiber goes a long way.

OTHER TOOLS

You will need a surface to work on. This is a matter of choice, but I prefer to use upholstery-grade foam, approximately 2 in (5 cm) thick. This foam in my photos is 8 in (20 cm) square, but use a size that suits you. At home, I use a wooden tray with a piece of foam cut to fit the bottom of it. Leave a few inches each side and you can use the space to stash your tools.

For jointing, I use dental floss. A surprising item, perhaps, but waxed floss is very easy to tie firmly. The knots hold well, it threads easily onto a needle and it's well priced! Just be sure you don't get flavored or other unusual kinds. Waxed ribbon floss is fine too.

You will need needles for sewing and jointing. I use a fine doll needle or a long darning needle. For beading, if you don't want to use a beading needle, find long darners or doll needles with small eyes so the beads will fit over them.

Threads come in many different varieties. I like crochet thread (fine) for attaching eye beads and embroidery thread split into three strands for everything else. Collect lots of colors for your stitched details, such as noses and claws, but use black for attaching beads.

Beads in smaller sizes can be hard to source. I like to use ⅛ in (3 mm) round black beads generally, though ³⁄₁₆ (4 mm) is good for slightly larger bears, or when I want a more wide-eyed look. Don't use seed beads, as these are not round but have flat sides.

The fiber pictured above, from left: merino (white) with angora (pink); a sea-green blend (Corriedale wool); the tangerine is a blend of merino and silk; the natural brown is an undyed Romney fiber; and the white is Corriedale wool.

CHRISTMAS ORNAMENT

This project will teach you the basic principles of needle felting and give you a feel for how the wool can be manipulated. You can make more than a Christmas ornament with these instructions, and once you have finished your first attempt you can experiment with other colors and designs.

YOU WILL NEED:

+ Core fiber
+ Colored fiber for main color
+ Fiber in assorted colors for decoration
+ Felting needles and foam mat
+ Ribbons and beads to decorate
+ Needle and thread to hang ornament

TO BEGIN

Take a length of core fiber and begin rolling it into a tight ball, winding as you would a ball of yarn. If you haven't wound a ball of yarn before, all you need to do is keep turning and placing the wool so that it is not all going in the same direction. Keep winding and turning until it is approximately the size of a tennis ball. You may need to add more fiber as you go. (Because you are winding the wool tightly, the finished piece won't get much smaller as you felt it.) Once you are happy with the size, you can start to needle the fiber.

HOW TO NEEDLE FELT

Always begin with the largest needle. Keep in mind that larger needles are also often longer. If you have a few needles and they have a number guide, then the lower the number the larger the needle. You can also test them by trying them in the fiber. The smaller needles will seem ineffectual at the start of a project.

Begin by poking the needle straight in and out of the ball of fiber. Do not bend or change the direction of the needle once embedded in the ball.

Work using your elbow as the pivot point and not your wrist, as you will break more needles pivoting at the wrist and your wrist will become sore.

You want your project to be smooth and even, so turn your work frequently. Don't ever leave your project in one place on your foam, even when making a flat piece such as an ear, or it will become firmly attached!

This is the core of your project. Keep poking and turning evenly. I usually do five or six pokes in an area and then turn, doing another five or six pokes, until I have worked over the entire piece. If you notice any bumps appearing, just target them with a few extra pokes.

You can also roll the ball firmly in your palms to help it keep a round shape. Then work on it again with your needle. After you get about halfway through this stage, you will see the reason for having a multi-needle tool. They are very useful for both starting projects and for larger pieces as the work felts down much more quickly.

! Do not use your needles for anything else! They break very easily. Don't use them to pick things out of the fiber or for anything non-felting related as they will just snap.

How firm your piece should be is a personal thing. You want it quite firm so that you can decorate it without losing its round shape. If you felt it too hard, however, it won't be easy to attach more fiber. This is one of those lessons you can only learn by doing. I suggest that you don't just make one ornament — make a bunch of them in different sizes and patterns, and experiment with your decorations. The more you make, the more you will learn.

ADDING COLOR

Next, cover the ball you have felted with your chosen main color. I like to work with fine merino wools for these balls as they create a smooth surface and it is easier to get sharp patterns. Other fibers will leave a fuzzy surface. But work with whatever you have. You can always trim the fuzzy bits off later.

Take a handful of colored wool and mix the fibers up. Most fiber from commercial suppliers will come in a long rope. This means all the fiber is laying in one direction. If you felt with it this way, it will never get as firm or as smooth as when the fiber is laying in different directions. Pull the fiber apart, teasing the strands and mixing them as you go. The better it is mixed, the better your finish will be.

Once mixed, make a nest in your hand and gently wrap the nest around the felted ball. Start poking to attach it to the core.

You may find bald areas as you felt. Just add pinches of mixed fiber over these thin spots as you work. It is better to add them as you go rather than at the very end as they will blend in better.

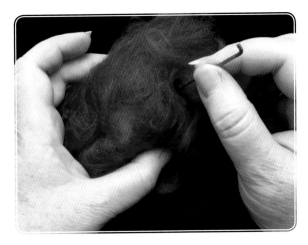

DECORATING YOUR ORNAMENT

When the outer layer is evenly felted, you can start to decorate. This is a chance to use your imagination. Go online and look up Christmas images to inspire you. You can add simple lines, zigzags or swirls. Or you can make snowflakes, snowmen or landscapes. If you want it to be more three-dimensional, you can felt shapes a little on your foam mat before attaching them to the ball (see ornaments in the main photo).

For this snowflake design, take small pinches of white merino and twist them to make little ropes.

With your finer needle, poke one end of the rope into the ball until it disappears. Then lay the rope along the surface of the ball and using your larger needle felt along it to make a straight line. If some lines are too short, you can make them longer with another pinch of fiber. Tidy them up by working along the line at the very edge so that all the loose white fibers are tucked away. Don't work too deeply.

Do this a number of times, with each line meeting in the middle and all evenly attached. You can then add arrows at the end of each point to give it a lovely snowflake effect.

You could do any pattern with this technique. Spirals look wonderful or you can add letters.

When you have added your design, work the entire surface with your finer needle to get a smooth finish. You will see the difference in the grades of needle when you change down as the holes in the fiber will be smaller, the needle will slip through your project more easily and the finish will be even.

To complete this project, you can add beads, ribbons and thread to hang (see diagram below). The photograph below shows different examples of what you can do, but search around for more ideas.

ADDING THREAD TO HANG

Take a long piece of medium-weight thread such as embroidery thread and thread your long needle with a single strand.

Enter the top of the ball (a) and leave a long tail of thread. Come out at one side (b). Poke the needle back in at *exactly* the same place. Now go across to the other side of the ball (c) and take the needle out and in at exactly the same place, coming out at the top again. Tie the ends to the length you wish.

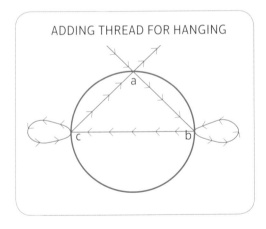

ADDING THREAD FOR HANGING

Once you have completed this project, you can use these ideas to make other decorated items. You could make fruit to decorate a table, or you could turn the ball into a little cartoon character for a child to play with. Animals love wool balls, and you can make a cat or dog toy in the same way.

If you are making decorated balls for children or animals you can also wet felt them. Wet felting creates a smoother surface and the ball is a little sturdier for rough play. Wet felting is easily done. Place the finished felted project into a piece of stocking (an old knee-high will do), tie a knot in it and throw into a warm wash with your other washing! Dry in a warm, sunny spot.

CUPCAKE PINCUSHION

With this project you will learn more about manipulating fiber, as you will be creating a different shape to that of the round Christmas ornament. You will also learn how to make a flat base so that your cupcake sits nicely on a flat surface.

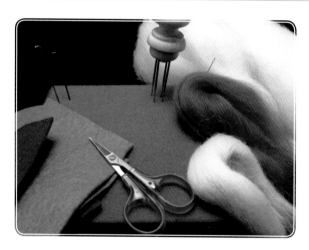

YOU WILL NEED:

- Core fiber in any color
- Fiber in "cake" colors, such as chocolate, vanilla, or strawberry
- Fiber for the "frosting"
- Commercial felt for the cupcake "cases"
- Ribbon and beads (optional)
- Foam
- Large and small felting needles

Select and wind your core fiber as you did for the ornament. However, as you wind for this project, try to make more of a cylinder shape. Squeeze and shape with your hands, rolling to give it sides.

When you are happy with the size of your cupcake ball, begin felting with your larger needle (or multi-needle tool). Remember to keep poking and turning the fiber so that it doesn't stick to the foam and so that the shape will begin to firm up evenly. You want the shape to taper away at the bottom slightly so that you can create a flat base for the pincushion to stand on.

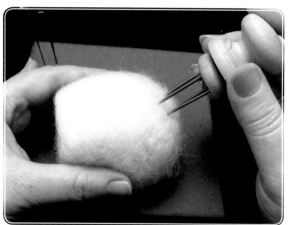

To make the bottom flat, sit the cupcake on its top and felt around in a circle, working the base evenly. You can shape the piece with your hands too. To get the base flat, press it firmly onto your table and then quickly felt the area to hold the shape.

To get a nice rounded top, just work evenly all over as you did for the Christmas ornament.

The pictures give you a shape to aim for. But remember, it is your first time, so don't expect perfection! As with the ornaments, I recommend you make a few pincushions to improve your technique.

COVERING THE CORE

Now you want to give your cupcake a color. You can either cover the core as you did for the ornament (see page 13), or you can cover the top and bottom only as shown here as this is all that will be seen above the the felt case.

Take some fiber to cover the top and mix it well. Rub it in your hands to make it flat, then felt it a little on your foam using the larger needle (or multi-needle tool). Remember to turn it a few times so you get a thick, even covering. You don't want too many bald patches. As you are working with a smaller amount of fiber, you can do this. It would not be easy to cover a large ball this way.

Place your lightly felted top onto the cupcake core and work with the large needle from the center outward so that the covering comes down evenly over the top of the cupcake shape.

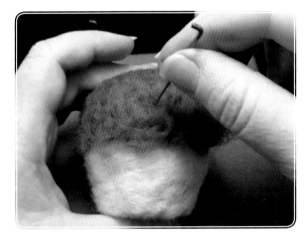

You don't need to work this for too long as you will be putting another layer over it. Just make sure that it is smooth and the edges are well attached, as they are most likely to show when finished.

Do the same again to cover the base of the cupcake. Ensure you keep the surface smooth so that your cupcake will stand easily and not wobble when on a flat surface.

THE CUPCAKE CASE

When your cupcake is smooth, you are ready to add the case. You can choose any color you prefer (see some other color options in the photo on page 22).

Using the cupcake as a guide, wrap a strip of felt around it, with an overlap of at least ¼ inch (5–6 mm). Mark where you will cut the felt. Also mark the bottom edge, again allowing a ¼-inch overlap. Cut out your felt case. Each cupcake is different so it is a good idea not to cut the felt before you start.

Holding the strip, begin felting along the edge to ensure it will stay hidden. Needle up and down in a straight line a few times.

Once the felt is well attached, take it around the cupcake and overlap it to cover the other end. Keep working back and forth along the join to form an indentation. This will help to hide the join and blend in with the other lines you are about to make.

Now you can start making the "ruffles" by working lines as evenly spaced as you can around the case. As long as you felt in a straight line, and keep going over the same place, you should get a nice even indentation. You can also run your fingernail firmly along

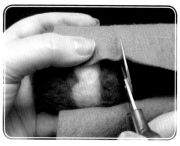

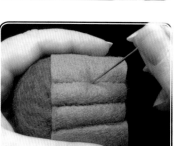

the indentation to help hide the holes left from the needle and to help straighten the lines. Now you are ready to put on the frosting.

FROSTING

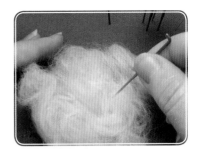

Take the frosting color and mix it well, then arrange it into a circle on your foam. Try not to make it too thin or it will be see-through in places. Also, make it just a little larger than needed to cover the top of your cupcake.

Needle the frosting fiber repeatedly on your foam with a large needle, remembering to turn over each time the surface has been evenly poked. You don't want it sticking to the foam! Keep working it on your foam, bringing the edges in to make them even and tidying up the flyaway fibers.

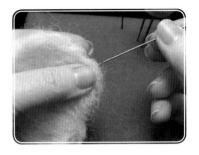

To make an even edge, hold the piece between your fingers and felt into the edge. This takes some practice but it is a technique that you will use later on a much smaller piece so it is good to try it now. Remember, you don't want a perfect circle — frosting can dribble down the sides.

Once you are happy with the size and shape of the frosting, attach it to the cupcake. Lay the frosting over the top and needle from the center outward.

When you reach the edge, travel along it with your needle to tidy up and create a nice "drippy" look. Keep working like this, needling all over the top until firm. Then change down to the smaller needle once the larger one becomes harder to use.

For this project I have made the frosting smaller than the top of the cupcake, but a nice effect can be gained from bringing the frosting down over the edge of the cupcake case (see page 17 for examples). You can experiment by adding pieces of mixed fiber and blending them into the top. Have fun and see what you can create.

TOPPING

For this topping I chose to make a drizzle of caramel by creating a tiny rope in this gorgeous merino/silk fiber and placing it on top of the cupcake where I wanted it. This way I could see how it would look. Then with a few pokes to secure it, I felted along its length with the smaller needle.

Keeping the edges tidy is the trick with this style. Make sure you come in on an angle all along the rope so that it doesn't get too fat and untidy. I did it twice in two directions, but you can do anything you like!

Once you are happy with your frosting and case you may want to add beads to the top. If you have pearl-topped pins you can just use those for decoration.

When adding beads, make sure that you don't sew through your cupcake case as it will leave visible marks. Either just go through the top or go in and out of the bottom of the cupcake.

Tying a bow around the base looks very nice, or you may have other items you have collected which will work. On one of the examples below, I have also made a swirled frosting top. This was achieved by felting a long sausage of fiber and then attaching one end just above the case and working up, circling as you go.

NEEDLE-FELTED PIN

During this project you will learn how to work on a smaller scale. Up to now, the projects have been reasonably large, and the risk of poking yourself has been quite low! Now you will get a feel for working with much smaller pieces as this is a skill you will need when creating jointed bears and other critters.

YOU WILL NEED:

- Main fiber color
- Assorted colors and fibers
- Any ribbons, threads, beads, etc. for decoration
- Pin fixture or a small safety-pin
- Felting needles and foam mat

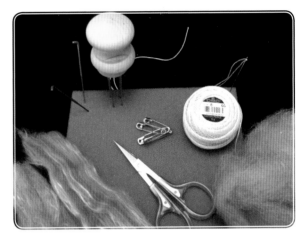

Start with a small amount of fiber, perhaps enough to fit into your closed fist. Mix the fiber well and then lightly roll it into a loose ball.

Begin felting this ball on your foam surface with your large needle or multi-needle tool. Keep poking and turning as you go until it begins to hold together. This is a good way to start a very sculpted project, because the fibers are a little firmer and are already beginning to hold a shape, which you can then sculpt as you wish. For this example, I am making an oval pin, but you could make any shape you like. Begin to flatten this ball out by felting on one side, then flipping over and felting the other side.

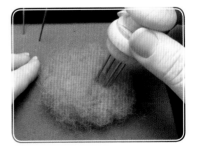

To make a nice edge on your pin, hold it between your fingers and felt around the sides with the needle going between your fingers into the middle. This can be a bit scary as you are likely to feel the needle, or even get poked by it, but by working carefully around the edge in this way you can create any shape you wish and get an even finish.

DECORATING YOUR PIN

For this pin, I chose a simple heart shape. I used two colors of merino fiber and hand mixed them to get the blend I wanted. This is very useful if you don't have a lot of fiber, or if you need a specific color for a project. Just mix and rub the fibers between your fingers to blend, then felt into a soft ball.

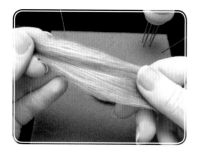 

To make the heart shape, pinch the fiber between your fingers and felt halfway along the edge to make a side. Turn over to make another side and create the point of the heart.

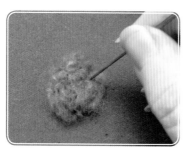 

To make the top of the heart, work the needle down into the fiber exactly where you want the center point of the heart to be. Use the finest needle you have and felt softly to coax the fiber into shape.

Check the fit and then begin felting the heart (or other decoration) onto the pin.

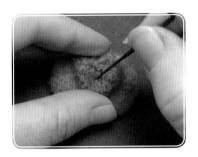

! Remember to start in the middle and work outward.

Then work along the edges to form defined lines and make your work stand out.

Keep sculpting all over with your fine needle.

Do not poke too deeply when felting smaller pieces as this will cause dents or holes that are then hard to reverse.

You can see in the photo above right that I worked down into the crease at the top of the heart to help keep the shape.

You can really use your imagination when decorating these pieces. You might want to felt on another shape or color decoration in a similar way to the heart, or do something more like the decoration of the Christmas ornament.

You can sew on beads or buttons, bows, flowers, etc. You could have things that hang from the pin such as chains, unusual yarns or ribbons.

Have fun making these pieces unique and interesting. You can add personal elements to create something very special to give as a gift.

FINISHING

To finish, sew a pin fixture or a safety-pin onto the back. This is easily done and you can use knots as they won't be seen. Just make sure that you don't take your thread through to the front and that your safety-pin is hidden and sewn on securely.

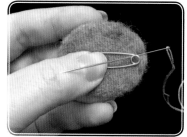
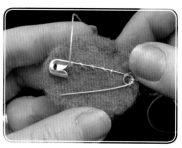

These pins make fantastic and very personal gifts and you will love sharing what you have created with family and friends. Small projects such as these are also a great way to learn from the fiber, and to get a feel for different textures and color blends. They also allow you to experiment with adding other items to your needle felting. All this will be of use to you later on.

ANIMAL HEAD KEYCHAIN OR PHONE CHARM

This project will teach the basics for making a ball-shaped bear's head, including how to attach felted ears, a muzzle and nose. You will also learn how to add the eye beads correctly — a very important technique.

For this project there is no core, as was used in the Christmas ornament. Cores aren't used for the bears in the later projects either, as the body parts are too small.

These little balls can have loops added and can be used for many things apart from keychains and phone charms. And cats love playing with these felted balls!

YOU WILL NEED:

- Main color fiber
- Complementary colored fiber for ears and features
- Eye beads — I used 1/8 in (3–4 mm) beads
- Long sewing needle
- Black thread for eye attachment
- Store-bought phone lariat, jump ring or heavy thread — whatever you would like to attach it to
- Felting needles and foam pad

Take a length of fiber and wind it into a ball, as in earlier projects. This ball should be a little smaller than for the Christmas ornament. You don't want the head to be too big if it is being used as a keychain or phone charm.

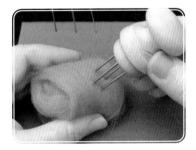

You want a smooth surface, so try to fluff the outer layer with your fingers so that there aren't any lines or creases. If these form as you are felting, you can needle felt small patches over the top to hide them.

Felt the ball until it is reasonably firm and ready for attaching the other pieces. Hopefully by now you are getting a feel for how firm your work should be. For this ball, you need it to have some give when squeezed but you don't want it to flatten out.

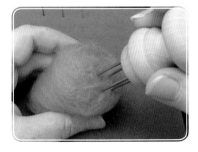
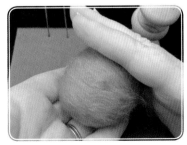
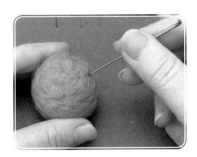

EARS

Take a small portion of fiber for the ears. Mix and roll well and then divide into two equal balls.

Needle these balls until they are holding their shape. Then flatten them and needle again, remembering to flip them over as you go so that they don't felt onto the foam. You may need to flip them three or four times.

Once they begin to firm up and stay flat, take them between your fingers and, using the smaller needle, carefully felt around three-quarters of the edge. Needling around the edge will make the ear tidy and even. Don't felt all the way around, as you want a portion of the ear to be left unfelted. This is where you attach the ear to the head.

Once both ears are finished you can attach them. To do this, hold the ear in place, with the loose fiber edge against the head.

Needle along the back of the ear with your bigger needle. Go back and forth a few times.

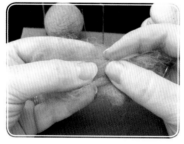
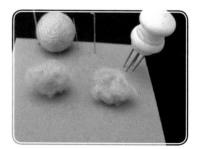
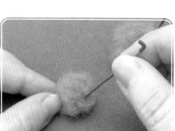
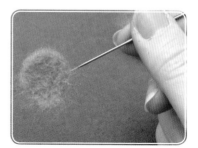

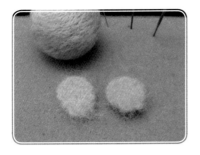 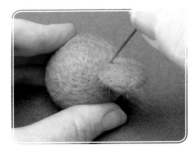

 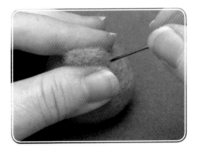

Working along the front and back of the ear with a smaller needle is especially useful when you are working with two different colors as it helps to keep the edge tidy.

Then pinch the ear between your fingers and go through the edge of the ear down into the head. Work back and forth here also.

Work along the front of the ear as you did for the back. Do the same again with the smaller needle to tidy the surface.

Add the other ear in the same way. I like to add the second ear before the first one is completely finished so that I can felt them at the same time and get the size and shape more even.

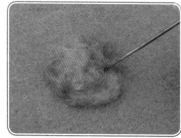
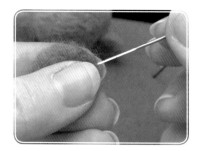

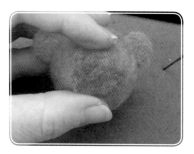
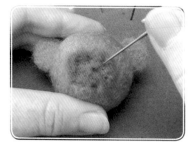

MUZZLE

Taking the color you would like for the muzzle, remember to mix it well and then felt it very loosely into a ball before flattening it into an oval or circle.

Felt both sides on your foam pad, remembering to turn often. The finer needle often works better for small pieces such as this.

Work around the edge to create a smooth shape, and then felt it directly onto the ball below where the eyes will be.

Start working from the center outward, then target the edges to keep them tidy. Work all over until smooth.

EYES

Before adding the eye beads, you first need to make eye sockets. Making these sockets allows the beads to sink back into the head a little and avoids a bug-eyed finish.

First, ensure you have accurately judged where you want the eye to be. You can mark this with a pen as the mark will be covered by the bead.

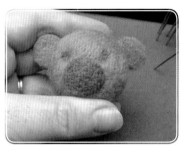

To make the socket, take your larger needle and simply felt in one place. Depending on your bead size you may want to enlarge the dent by moving outward in a circular motion to make a larger socket.

When you have made both sockets, thread your long sewing needle with approximately 12 in (30 cm) of black thread. You are using this single strand only to attach the beads.

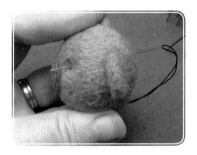

Start by coming through the back of the head and bringing the point of the needle out of one eye socket. Then pull the thread through until it just disappears at the back of the head.

Take the point of the needle back into the socket and out the back of the head again. Do not pull the thread too firmly at this stage.

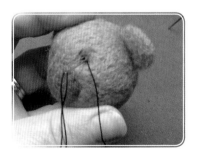

Take another pass through from the back of the head, ensuring you go back into the head at exactly the same place the thread was coming out. In this way you won't be making a stitch, so the thread should remain invisible at the back.

Coming out of the socket, this time give the thread a tug. If it feels very firm you can add the bead, but if not just make another pass through from front to back and then back to front. Pull again; it should be firm enough now.

Add the bead onto the thread and then take the point of the needle back into the socket and out of the head as before. Slowly pull the thread through, checking the bead as it can tangle.

Pull firmly, and the bead should sink into the socket you have made.

Do the same on the other side using the same thread, remembering first to anchor it through the eye socket before adding the bead.

Once both beads are firmly in place you will want to anchor the thread off. This is done instead of making knots, which are very fiddly and usually end up being visible and needing patches of fiber to hide them.

To anchor off, take the needle in at the point where the thread exits the head. Come out anywhere at the back of the head and then enter in the same place coming out somewhere different, though still at the back of the head. This method will ensure the thread is invisible. You will get small indentations but they will be less obvious at the back of the head.

Do this three or four times. Be careful not to pull too hard and not to make stitches. Then, cut the thread under tension and it should disappear into the fiber.

If there are dents, you can felt the area with your smaller needle to flatten the surrounding fibers. You can also rub the dents with your fingernail to rough the area up and then felt it lightly again.

NOSE

Take a pinch of your chosen nose color and roll it into a little ball.

Needle it with your small needle and then pop it straight onto the muzzle. Lightly felt the piece to create the shape you would like.

Work around the edge to keep it clean and tidy.

A LITTLE EXTRA

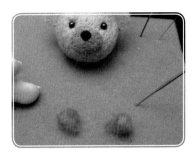

After finishing this bear's face, I decided that he needed some more color to finish him off. So I added a contrast color to the inside of his ears — using the same fiber as I did for his muzzle.

I could have done this before I attached the ears if I had planned it in advance but the beauty of felting is that you can add things later if you feel you can improve your piece.

The ear linings are very simple. First, pre-felt small pinches of fiber on your foam mat. Then add them to the ear, making sure that the fiber is pushed in against the head so that if it shrinks you don't finish with a gap between the head and the ear.

Work a nice edge with your fine needle and don't felt too deeply through the ear as the back of the ear will become speckled with the color from the front.

Be sure to use enough fiber to cover the whole inside of the ear. It will shrink a little as you felt and it can look wrong it if gets much smaller than the ear itself.

MAKING A LOOP

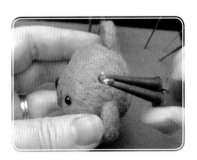

There are many ways that you can add a loop to the top of the head. Here I've just used a jump ring (from a jewelry making supplier) and deeply threaded it through the top of the head before closing it with my needle-nosed pliers.

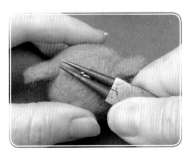

You can also just use thick thread as was done for the Christmas ornaments (see page 15) or sew a lariat to the top for attaching to your keys.

Ornamental Doll

The beginner projects taught you how to make a ball, decorate it and shape a base. With these skills, you will be able to create these little dolls. In the process, you will learn more about adding three-dimensional elements to your work as well as how to join a head to a body.

YOU WILL NEED:

- Core fiber
- Colored fiber for main color
- Fiber in assorted colors for decoration
- Felting needles and foam mat
- Black fiber for eyes
- White fiber for eyes
- Dental floss and sewing needle for jointing

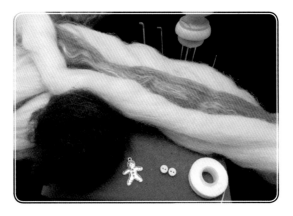

Start with the head, working as you did for the Christmas ornaments. Take a length of core fiber, and roll into a tight ball, winding the fiber as you would a ball of yarn. You may need to add more as you go.

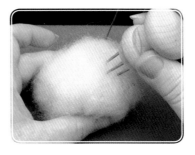

Keep going until it is roughly the size of a small orange. Please note that I have made a particularly large doll at just over 4½ in (12 cm). You are welcome to make a smaller one.

With your larger needle or multi-needle tool, start to needle the fiber to keep it in place and make a firm base for your top layer. Keep poking and turning, trying to keep the surface smooth. Remember you can also roll the ball firmly in your palms to help it keep a nice round shape. Then work on it some more with your needle.

MAKING THE BODY

Using just a little more fiber than you did for the head, roll another ball shape and needle felt on the foam. Felt with your multi-needle tool or large needle to get it fairly firm.

Begin to shape it as it firms up, much as we did for the cupcake pincushion project. You want one end to be flat so that it stands well and the other end to be a little more pointed to form a neck and shoulders.

Roll the piece in your hands once it is becoming firm to create a more oblong shape, then you can start sculpting. Keep using your large needle.

Remember, you can push the piece down onto the table to create a flat end, and then quickly needle the flat surface all over to keep it smooth.

If you are making a small doll you can do it without using a core at all, as covering small pieces is far too tricky to be worthwhile.

The main reason to use a core is to save your nicer fibers; cheaper, coarser wool also felts more quickly.

On small pieces, i.e., 2 in (5 cm) or less, the gain is minimal, so make it easier for yourself!

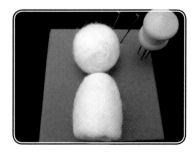

ADDING SKIN

Mix the skin color and create a little nest for the head.

Work over the surface with your large needle or multi-needle tool to attach the covering. You can add pieces of fiber as you go to cover any gaps you encounter.

Change down to your smaller needle to get the surface smooth as the larger needle will leave holes at this stage.

> Making a nice smooth surface can be time-consuming, especially on a piece the size I'm making here. But if you want a good finish it is worth the effort. Be methodical, but take breaks if you need to.

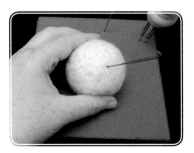

ADDING HAIR

For my doll, I made a side part with two little buns for her hair. You can do any hairstyle you like, including bangs and braids. It is fun to experiment.

Make a nest again, this time using the fiber in the hair color you have chosen.

Begin felting from the middle of the hair and work outward.

Before you get to the edges, you need to start to shape the style to see how it will work.

When I started this doll's hair it was going to be straight bangs across the forehead. But as I worked it began to look like a side part so I just went with it!

If there are gaps or the hairline isn't straight, you can still add bits of fiber and change the lines as you go. See photos above.

To make a part, just needle in a straight line through the hair to make an indentation and then go over it a few times. In the photos above and below, I am adding more fiber to the front of the hairline and turning it into a side-part style (left). Then I tidy the hairline (right).

The buns were made with small balls of mixed fiber. Felt them on your foam for a bit before adding them to the head. Make sure you check the placement from all angles before you felt them on. If you want the buns to be prominent, felt them quite firmly on your foam before attaching to the head as they then won't flatten so much.

Attach the buns by poking deeply with a large needle through the center of the bun and into the head. Work around that area a few times and then work over the whole bun quite deeply until it is well attached. Then change to a smaller needle to finish.

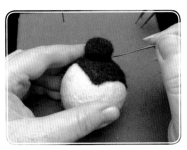 

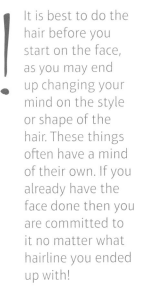

It is best to do the hair before you start on the face, as you may end up changing your mind on the style or shape of the hair. These things often have a mind of their own. If you already have the face done then you are committed to it no matter what hairline you ended up with!

ADDING A FACE

For this doll, I kept the face simple, but you can get as complicated as you like. She has just black dots for her eyes, with optional whites added for extra sparkle, and a little pink smile.

EYES

Roll two small equal-size dots, preferably using a merino fiber as this will give a smoother finish.

Felt them a little on your foam and then tack each one onto the head with a couple of pokes using your small needle to see if you are happy with the placement.

If the placement is working, carry on felting. But don't felt too deeply or the eyes will almost disappear, especially if the head isn't very firm.

Remember to start in the center and work your way out to the edge to keep the eye shape round and tidy.

MOUTH

For the mouth, mix a little pink fiber and then twist into a thread, just longer than you want the finished mouth to be. (Remember everything shrinks as you felt.)

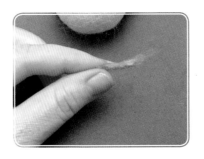

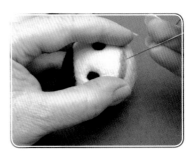

Attaching the mouth evenly across the face can be tricky. You might want to attach each end of the mouth first and then work on the curve. Or you can make a longer thread than you need and just cut off the extra bit when you are done.

Work along the thread using your fine needle to create a curved mouth. If the mouth is a little thick, you can work the edge with the needle pointing inwards and it will make the thread skinnier.

If you work lightly to start with you can always pull the mouth off if it is not working. Once you begin to felt firmly, you are more committed to it staying as it is.

You can add white to the eyes by taking two very tiny pinches of white fiber and mixing into little balls. These will be felted in the exact same place on each eye to create a light reflection effect — this makes the eyes look a little more alive. Using your smaller needle, felt the white straight onto the eye, as it is too small to pre-felt on your foam.

CLOTHING

I chose overalls for this doll, so the first step is to create the layer that goes underneath. Choose your color scheme, mix the fiber and place it over the top half of the body. Felt in place wth your large needle. This is the same technique as for the hair.

Then take the main color. Mix and pre-felt it a little, then wrap it around the rest of the body.

At first, it appears to almost cover the whole body, but remember the fiber shrinks as you felt! If you work from the top down, there will be ample left at the bottom for shrinkage.

 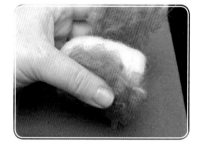

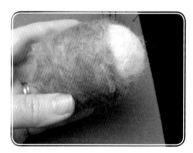 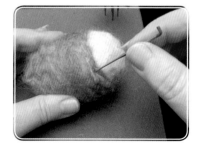

Once you are happy with the main part of the overalls, take even amounts of fiber and roll into little sausages for the straps.

Check the length (remember to make them a little longer than you need) — you can pull them longer if you need to as long as they aren't too skinny. Felt the straps a little on your foam to flatten and thicken them up.

Attach to the front of the overalls and work toward the back. You could cross the straps over or have them straight. If they end up too short you can always add a bit of fiber to lengthen them. This is why it is good to attach the front first, so that side is tidy.

To add a pocket (below), use another color (in this case, I used the same color as I did for the under layer). Mix and pre-felt it a little on your foam to create a circle. Then, holding it between your fingers, work the edges to create a square. Remember to make it a little bigger than the final size.

To attach, needle the sides and bottom edge deeply all the way along, leaving the top edge open to form the pocket. You can tidy the edges with scissors.

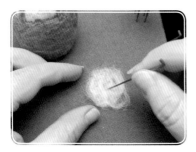

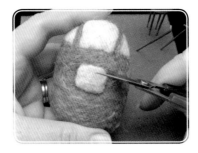

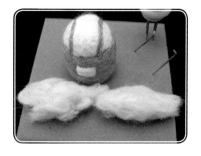  

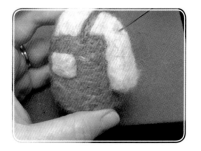  

ARMS

Take two equal pieces of fiber. Mix, roll and pre-felt them into little sausages. You don't want to make them too firm as you will be shaping and attaching them to the body. Get them as even in size as possible. At this stage, you can add fiber if one is a little smaller.

Tack them in place with a few pokes to check you are happy with placement and size.

Mine are sleeves, really, so I made the ends quite straight and wide. Also, they stick out a little from the body so that the hands have something to sit under.

> **!** If your arms are too thin or long, hold them upright and felt into the ends gently but deeply, this will fatten and shorten them.

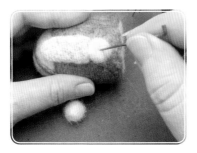

HANDS

For the hands, just mix little balls of skin-colored fiber, pre-felt on your foam and attach them straight on under the sleeves.

You can use your judgment on which size needle to use with these. If you are using a fine fiber, you may find that your large needle does not felt these small amounts very well. If you work entirely with a smaller needle, ensure that you work deeply to get a good attachment.

FINISHING TOUCHES

I was just about to attach the head when I decided the hair needed something pretty in it, so I made the little flower you see pictured right.

Take a pinch of pink (or whatever flower color you wish), and mix and pre-felt a tiny circle with your small needle. Then holding the circle, poke in at four places around the edge to make the four petals.

Take a few strands of lighter fiber for the center of the flower and make a little ball. Felt the petals straight on to the head with a few pokes in the center and then add the ball to the middle.

Working with these tiny amounts can be tricky. If the ball is too big just throw it away and make a smaller one. Don't try to make it work if you aren't happy, as odds are the ball will look huge and cover up most of the petals!

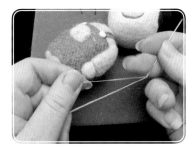

JOINTING

You will joint the doll in a similar way to the triangle method used for adding string to the Christmas ornament in the first project. This is because the body is too long for a needle to go right through.

Take a length of floss approximately 10 in (30 cm) long. Thread an inch or so (3–4 cm) through your sewing needle.

Take the needle upward from the center of the neck to the top of the head. Leave a long tail hanging out the bottom of approximately 3 in (10 cm) to tie off with. (I like to work the threads at the joint so that they can be tied off together and the ends buried. This keeps everything looking tidy, as you will see.)

Take the needle back into the head in exactly the same spot you came out of. This reduces the indentation in the top of the head. You will always get some, but it can be kept to a minimum.

Come out at the neck next to the thread that is already there. In this way you won't risk the thread pulling itself out and your head falling off! Pull the needle right through so it is ready to go into the body.

Now take the needle in through the neck on the body and out one side, preferably just behind the arm as this will make a little dent.

If you have made a very small doll, you can take the thread straight through the body from the neck and out the bottom. Then take the needle back in at the bottom and through to the top of the head to tie off. This is how the bears' heads are joined.

Go back into and through the body and out the other side, again behind the arm if possible. Now take the needle back into the same hole again and out through the neck by the other thread. Remove the needle.

You should now have the head and body joined by one thread and two pieces to tie off next to each other.

Tie the first half of a knot, pull firmly and check everything is lined up nicely. If not, at this stage you can remove the floss and start again. If it is looking good, finish tying the knot, flip over and tie another knot on the other side.

You can now take the two threads, put them back on the needle (cut to the same length first) and enter the body at the neck between the two pieces (at the center of the joint).

Take the needle out somewhere in the body and, holding the floss under tension, cut it right against the fiber so that it will go back in and not be seen.

As I mentioned earlier, this doll is rather large but I wanted the photos to be easy to follow. You can make your doll any size you wish, and create entire little families for children to play with or a lovely collection for display. Look online for ideas for dressing and decorating your creations.

BASIC BEAR

The basic bear brings together the various elements taught in the previous projects — from the first felted ball to the ornamental doll. If you have worked through these, you will have the skills needed to create this lovely little bear. The basic bear has five joints (head, arms and legs), all done with thread and felted very firmly so the bear will last a lifetime. I hope you enjoy bringing your little bears to life!

With needle felting, no two bears are exactly the same, even when you want them to be! So it is a good idea to work through this project a number of times, perhaps changing a little something each time. You could try different color combinations, or change the placement of the eyes and ears (see pages 116 for color ideas and 106 and 110 for eyes and ears).

This is the stage where you figure out what your unique style will be. Try everything, search for ideas and experiment. You may not always love the results, but you could be surprised. And if we don't always love our creations, someone else will! Just enjoy what you do and your love for the craft will always show in your work.

The instructions for this project are written as a two-color bear, but you can mix and match, use all one color or go wild! The great thing with this craft is how little fiber you need to use, so if you make pink arms for your blue bear and then decide you don't like the look, just pop them aside and make new ones. You wouldn't believe the bag of "spare parts" I had when I was first learning to felt. In fact I still have them and one day I'll make a little Frankenstein bear with them!

Cute little basic bears showing some simple color combinations and different feet styles.

YOU WILL NEED:

- Colored fiber in two complementary colors
- Embroidery thread for stitched details
- 2 black eye beads (1/8 in or 3–4 mm) across
- Dental floss for jointing
- Felting needles and foam mat
- Long sewing needle
- Scissors

MAKING THE HEAD

Take two pieces of fiber, one larger than the other. The larger piece should just fill your fist and the smaller one should be a quarter of that size. These will be your head and muzzle.

Beginning with the head, mix the fibers and then roll them into a soft ball. Start felting with your largest needle or multi-needle tool. Make sure you poke and turn constantly as you work, to keep your ball round.

Keep working until the piece is firm and begins to resist the needle. (As you felt, it becomes more difficult to push the needle in. I call this "resisting the needle").

Work on the muzzle in the same way. When both pieces are firm, join together as follows.

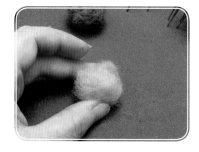

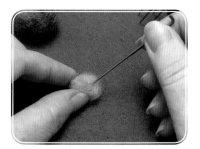

ATTACHING THE MUZZLE TO THE HEAD

The muzzle needs to sit at the same level as the bottom of the head, or as close as you can get to this.

Place the head and muzzle on your foam. Holding them in place, make deep pokes through the muzzle (smaller ball) and into the head (larger ball).

Once the muzzle is well attached, I like to work across the join at the top to keep it tidy.

Felt evenly around the entire muzzle. If you are working with two colors it is especially important to keep the join neat.

Once you are happy that the muzzle has attached well, check the placement. Nine times out of ten it will have moved from where you wanted it to be. But never fear, we have a trick up our sleeve!

At this stage of felting, the pieces are quite malleable and you can pinch, squeeze and roll to coax them into the shapes you want. If the muzzle has traveled up the head, you can press the bottom of the head up while pulling the muzzle down.

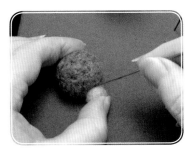

You can also shape the head a little at this point. I find pressing the head above the muzzle where the eyes will be can create a nice forehead.

After doing this, felt again using the smaller needle and felting all over to ensure the muzzle stays in position. You may need to do this a couple of times.

But before the head gets too firm, we will make and attach the ears.

MAKING AND ATTACHING THE EARS

Take a large pinch of fiber and mix. Split into two equal parts and roll between your fingers to check if they are even. Lightly felt the balls on your foam with the large needle.

When they begin to firm up, you need to flatten them. You can squeeze them flat and then felt each side, remembering to flip them over so they don't attach to the foam.

Next, shape these flat balls into more of an ear shape. Pinch one between your fingers and use your smaller needle to slowly but deeply felt around the sides. Leave a small section unfelted as this will be where you attach the ear to the head.

Hold the ears against the head to check placement. You can do a few pokes into each one to tack it in place and they will still come off if you're not happy (different placements give your bear different looks, see page 110). It's also better if they are slightly larger than you would like at this stage, as they will shrink down when we attach them to the head.

 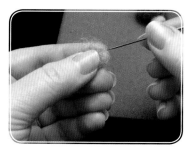

When you are satisfied with the position of the ears, you can work across the back of the ear, needling back and forth along the join.

Then pinch the ear between your fingers and work around the top of the ear, right through and into the head.

 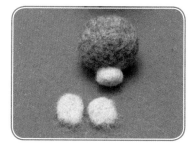

Work back and forth from one ear to the other to make sure they are the same size.

Getting both ears the same can be tricky but as long as they are a similar size you will be fine. If not make another one, or another pair if it's easier.

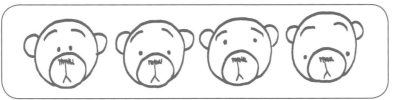

THE EYES

Where you place the eyes will determine much of the "character" of your bear. If you can't imagine how different placements will look, insert pins with beads on them in different positions on the face to see which you like best.

Once you have decided, make the socket by felting in one place. To make the socket bigger, work out from the center in a widening circle. Use your smaller needle for this. The socket should be just a little larger than the bead, so the eyes are not bulging.

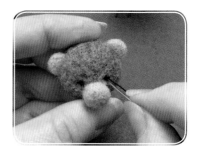

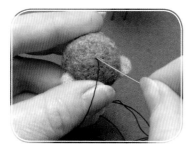

This step shows you how to anchor off your thread so that you don't use any knots in your work except to finish off the jointing.

Cut a length of black perle cotton and thread a single strand onto your sewing needle. Insert your needle into the back of the head, and take it out through one socket. Pull the thread through until the end just disappears. Then go back into the head from the socket and take the needle through and out the back of the head again.

As the needle is going in at the same point the thread comes out, no visible stitch is made. After three passes give the thread a tug to see if it is well anchored. You can always make another pass if there is still movement.

! When finished, check that your beads are sitting well. You may find that the bead hole is visible. This doesn't look good, so take your sewing needle and place the end into the hole. Move the bead around so that the hole is no longer seen.

With the needle on the socket side of the head, thread on the bead and slide it down to the end. Now take the needle back into the socket and out at the back of the head. Guide the thread through to avoid knots.

When the bead is in the socket, pull the thread firmly. Then take your needle back into the head and out the other socket. Add a bead, take the needle back through the socket and out the back of the head as before. Pull firmly and take the thread back and forth through the back of the head to anchor off. Cut the thread under tension by pulling it as you cut right up against the fiber.

MAKING THE NOSE

For the embroidered details on your bears, you can use colored thread instead of the black for a different look. However, it pays not to use a thread that is too fine, especially if you are making a large nose, as it will take a lot longer and can look messy. If you are using stranded embroidery cotton, use three strands.

Begin by anchoring the thread, as shown earlier, ending with the thread coming out at the base on one side of the nose.

Take a stitch into the top of the muzzle, directly above where the thread started, then come out again next to the first stitch.

You are making a looping stitch that goes in at the top and out at the bottom.

Work all the way across the muzzle and then back again. You can keep going back over the nose three or four times if you wish. This makes a thick nose with a little dimension to it rather than a flat one.

When you are happy with the nose size and thickness have your next stitch end at the bottom middle of the nose. This is the point where you will make a line down from the nose to create a little mouth. Essentially it is an upside-down Y shape.

I like to lay the thread down to see where it will finish. This allows me to make sure the thread is straight and that I am happy with the expression it creates.

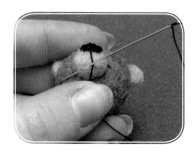

Take your needle in at the bottom of the line above where the mouth will be. Your needle will go in at the middle and out on one side, then back in at the middle and out on the other side.

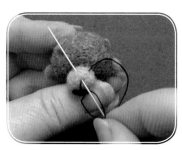

Take the last stitch in at the middle again and then back out through the head as shown.

Anchor off through the back of the head.

I hope you are pleased with the head you have created. It is a rather important part of the project, and if you are not completely satisfied you can always make another. Even after a bear has been finished, I have been known to cut off its head and put another one on if I haven't been completely happy with the look!

MAKING THE BODY

The body really is as simple as it looks. It is basically just an elongated egg shape.

Take a large handful of fiber, similar to the size used for the head or slightly more. (Remember quantity is very hard to judge at the start. Don't worry too much and remember less is more as it is easy to add fiber but quite hard to make a piece smaller.)

Start mixing the fiber and rolling it into a loose ball. Begin felting with your large needle or multi-needle tool, poking and turning to keep it round.

As it begins to firm up, roll the piece firmly between your palms to form a fat sausage. Now you can needle one end to a point and the other end into a fat, round shape.

At this stage, you can manipulate the piece as we did with earlier shapes by pinching the point and poking the fat end with inward pokes to fatten it up.

Once the fibers start resisting the needle, change to your finer needle and keep poking evenly and turning to create a smooth finish.

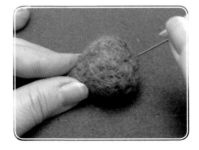

MAKING THE LEGS

When making limbs you want them to be the same size, so for both the arms and legs always work them in pairs.

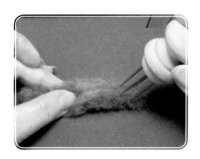

Take a large handful of fiber and mix. Pull apart into two equal pieces, roll into a ball and then firmly roll into a sausage. Do both legs and then compare sizes. You can add or remove fiber to ensure they match.

Begin working the leg from one end only. This helps to ensure both are of equal size as you can still add and remove fiber as you go.

Starting at one end, poke and turn the sausage, working down just over half the length. To keep it thick, come in on the end, felting slowly and deeply into the length of the leg. Then go back to felting across the width. This helps to ensure the fiber is well felted in all directions.

Change to your finer needle and work until the leg feels firm.

Felt both legs to the same stage. Now compare the loose ends and check that the felted ends are the same length.

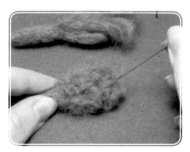

Once you are happy, you can move onto the next step. If not, you can add and remove pinches of fiber at the loose end until the legs match.

Using your larger needle begin felting the loose ends lightly all over so that they compact and thicken up. The leg will begin to look a bit like a lollipop. (They are still the same size? Good!) This large end will become the foot. Remember at this stage it will look a lot larger than the final foot, but it will shrink as you felt it.

Fold the pre-felted foot over the leg and needle the heel area a number of times. Once it is holding its shape, flip the leg over, putting the foot flat on the foam. Needle inwards from different directions to shrink the foot down.

Flip over and place the leg down the side of the foam, working the bottom of the foot to make it nice and flat. If the foot seems a little flat and soft, you can pinch it between your fingers gently and work around the edge as we did for the ears. Keep checking the feet together to get them as similar as possible.

When you are happy with their shape, change down to your finer needle and finish firming them up.

Now that your legs are done you might like to add stitched claws. To do this, firmly anchor a length of thread into the foot, bringing the thread out at the point where you want one of the claws to finish (on the bottom of the foot). Take a stitch into the top of the foot, coming out again at the bottom of the foot in the place where the second claw should be. Do this until you have three or four claws spaced evenly along the end of the foot. Anchor off and then do the other foot.

Making Arms

Take a handful of fiber as you did for the legs (though slightly smaller for the arm pieces). Mix it and split into two equal pieces. Roll them into two balls and then two sausage shapes.

Start needle felting at one end with the larger needle or multi-needle tool and work down about three-quarters the length of the sausage. Remember to needle felt in from the end as well to ensure that the arms are not too skinny.

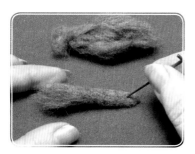

Keep working with the large needle until the fiber resists, then change down to the finer needle.

Check both arms are in proportion to each other and the bear's body before pre-felting the paws into a semi-ball shape.

Flatten these ends, flipping over from time to time and taking the needle around the end as you pinch it between your fingers.

Before the piece becomes too firm, put in the bend for the elbow. All you need to do is hold it in an L-shape on the foam pad and felt the shape in place.

Change to the finer needle to finish the piece. If you wish, anchor a thread and make claws for the bear's paws as you did for the feet (see previous page).

Jointing

Thread jointing is a simple but effective way to joint felted projects together. Because there are no metal joints you don't need extra tools and supplies. And once you get the hang of it, this method of jointing is easy, firm and makes for a well-finished bear.

To begin, lay your bear out on the foam with all the parts laying in the correct order. In this way, you can easily see where and how the limbs connect. For thread jointing, we use dental floss. A surprising material, perhaps, but floss is ideal because the waxed thread is strong and holds knots tightly. It is similar to traditional threads used for larger bears but not as thick, so it works well for our purposes. Cut roughly 12 in (30 cm) of floss and thread one end onto your long sewing needle. Only take an inch or so (2–3 cm) of thread through the needle so that you can easily remove the needle later.

Step 1: Attaching the Head

Poke the needle into the bottom of the head where the neck would be and take it out through the top. Pull the floss through leaving about 3 in (10 cm) hanging from the bottom of the head.

Now enter the top of the head in exactly the same place as the needle came out. Take the needle back through the head to come out next to the thread left at the neck. This way you will make as small a dent as possible in the top of the bear's head, and by exiting next to the thread the floss won't just pull out (making the head fall off).

You now have a head on a string. Next, take the needle from the top of body, also where the neck would be, and travel right down to the bottom, taking the needle right through the body and gently pulling the thread until the head and body are touching. Go back through again, exactly where you came out, and take the needle up to the neck next to the thread that's there. Pull through and remove the needle, leaving the floss ready to tie.

Making a firm half knot you can turn the head to see if it will sit nicely. Until this point the body doesn't really have a front. I like to add things like a belly button or any other tummy features last, or at least after the head is attached, so I have the head sitting at the best angle.

If you are happy with the placement of the head, keep the thread tight and finish the knot. Then flip the bear over and tie a second knot. I always do two — better to be totally sure that the joints will last.

Don't cut those threads yet. You need to bury the ends so they don't slip and can't be seen. Thread them both back onto the needle and take the needle in between the head and neck joint. Enter the body and exit anywhere in that piece.

Holding the thread tightly, cut against the body so the floss will disappear back into it.

The head and body are now attached. Time to add the limbs.

STEP 2: ATTACHING THE LEGS

Looking at your bear laid out on the table, think about where the legs touch the body. What will be the inside and outside of each limb? Where on the belly do they go?

Thinking about these areas, take your needle, threaded with 12 in (30 cm) or so of floss and insert it on the inside of one leg and take it through and out the other side. Remember to leave a 3-in (10-cm) tail to tie at the end.

Then insert the needle NEXT to the thread, making a small stitch, and come out next to the tail you left. So you now have a leg threaded onto your floss.

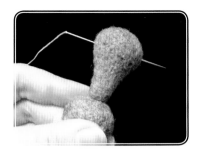
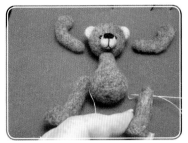

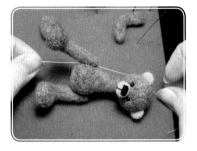

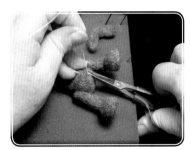

Take your needle in again at the matching point on the body where the leg will go. Take the needle right through ensuring it is straight and level across the body. Pull the floss through so that the first leg is now touching the body.

Enter the second leg at the inside coming through to the outside, taking a stitch as before. As your needle exits the leg take it into the body next to the other thread and come out the other side. Pull the thread through and remove your needle.

You now have both legs attached. Check that the feet point the right way (and yes I did get a few backwards at the start!) and that your two threads are next to each other ready for tying off.

As with the head, pull firmly and tie half a knot. Check everything looks good and if happy finish the knot, flip over and tie another on the other side.

Cut the threads at the same length, thread back onto the needle and then bury in the body, entering at the joint where they came out. Remember to cut under tension.

> The reason we take a stitch in the limbs and not the head or body is because it's a much smaller piece and the likelihood of the thread pulling right out is therefore higher. Taking a stitch ensures they are more firmly anchored onto the floss.

STEP 3: ATTACHING THE ARMS

Joint your arms in exactly the same way as the legs.

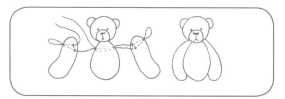

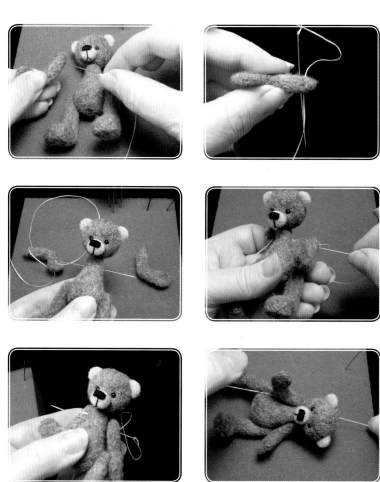

For this project, I made the entire bear and then jointed it.
This was so you could see how the bear would all fit together.
I generally attach each part as I go, starting with the head.
I find that it helps to create the character and stops pieces
from being lost!

You have finished your first jointed bear. Well done! There is so much more to learn and so many ways for you to experiment. I hope this project has sparked more ideas for you to try. And I hope that you start pulling out gorgeous colored fibers to mix and match together, and that you will try to incorporate what makes you unique into your work to make it unique too. Please go to the back of the book for more ideas on different color combinations, accessories and ideas for making your bears special.

ADVANCED BEAR

For this project, you can build on what you have already learned plus add new elements that are perhaps a little harder to do. But they make your work more interesting and unique to you. This bear has a one-piece head. When I first started needle felting I was told this was easier than a two-piece head but I have always had trouble with it. When I learned how to do two-piece heads I loved them and so kept doing those instead. However, I want you to learn how to do a one-piece as it involves more sculpting and you may prefer working this way. Also you will learn how to do whites under the eyes and use eyebrows to add expression. You will add toe pads, which are super cute, and make dropped paws, which require more sculpting but give a great look to your bears.

YOU WILL NEED:

- ◆ Fiber for main color, fiber for complementary color
- ◆ White fiber for under eyes
- ◆ Beads for eyes
- ◆ Felting needles
- ◆ Foam square

HEAD

Take a handful of mixed fiber and start out almost as though you are making a body. Begin felting the fiber into a ball with a large needle or multi-needle tool, then roll it a little in your hands to form an oblong shape.

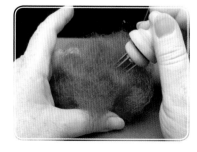

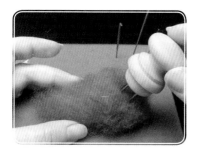
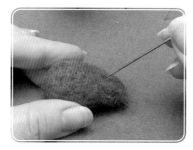

Keep working with the multi-needle tool or large needle to felt the fiber until it begins to firm and take an egg shape. You don't want the shape too long, but it does need a rounded "head" end and a pointed "muzzle" end.

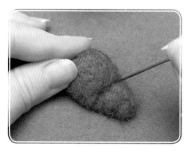

When it becomes semi-firm and springy when squeezed, form the muzzle by felting across in a line about one-quarter of the way up from the pointed end. You will see that this instantly gives you more of a head shape. When you are happy with the proportions, begin to felt all over to help it keep this shape.

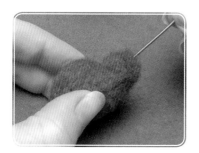

With this style of head, I find you need to keep manipulating the piece with your fingers to keep the muzzle in position.

Squeezing above the muzzle roughly where the eyes would be also helps to keep the definition in your piece.

Change down to your finer needle, but don't let it get too firm as you still need to add ears and make eye sockets.

You can make the muzzle quite pointed and fine or round it out for a chubbier shape. The main thing is not to lose the area where you will be putting the eyes.

EARS

The ears are made just as they were for the basic bear (page 56).

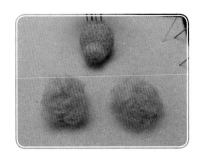

Take a large pinch of fiber and mix. Split into two equal parts and roll between your fingers to check that they are even. Lightly felt the balls on the foam.

When they begin to firm up, flatten them by squeezing them flat and then felting each side, remembering to flip them over so they don't attach to the foam.

Shape these flat balls into more of an ear shape by pinching between your fingers and using the smaller needle to slowly but deeply felt around the sides. Leave a small section unfelted as this will be where the ear is attached to the head.

Getting both ears the same can be tricky, but as long as they are a similar size you will be fine. If not, make another one, or another pair if it is easier. It is also better if they are slightly larger than you would like at this stage, as they will shrink down in the process of attaching them to the head.

Hold the ears against the head, and see where you like the look of them. You can do a few pokes into each one to tack it in place and they can still come off if you're not happy with placement. Where you put the ears can vary and will give your bear a different look (see page 110 for more on ear placement).

When the ears are in the right place you can be more vigorous with your poking. Work across the back of the ear, needling back and forth along the join. Then pinch the ear between your fingers and work around the top of the ear right through and into the head.

Work back and forth from one ear to the other to make sure they are the same size.

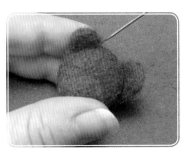

EYES

Make indentations for your eye beads by felting with the larger needle in one place where you want the socket to be. You can enlarge the size to suit the bead by felting in a little circle until the indent is deep enough.

When both sockets are done, anchor the thread by bringing the needle and thread back and forth through the head at the socket point. Come out at the socket and then enter the head again in the same place. Remember you don't want anything to be seen.

Pull firmly to be sure it is well anchored and then thread the bead and take the needle through the socket and out the back of the head.

Pull firmly again to ensure the bead sinks a little way into the head, then take the needle in from the back of the head and out of the other socket.

Repeat the process and anchor off by going back and forth through the head. (For more detailed photos on this process go to pages 57, Basic Bear.)

Cut under tension so that the thread end will disappear!

> **!** If you want to make black thread eyebrows and nose, and you have enough thread on your needle, don't anchor off, go straight from attaching the beads to sewing the nose and eyebrows.

NOSE

Just as was done on the basic bear, this bear has a sewn nose, and this style of head suits a much smaller nose than you can do on the two-piece head so keep it smaller and finer.

Either anchor off a new thread or continue with the one you are using from the eye bead attachment. Bring the thread out at the front of the muzzle, bottom left of where the nose will be.

Take a stitch into the top of the muzzle, above where the thread started, then come out again next to the first stitch. In this way you are making a looping stitch, in at the top, out at the bottom.

Work all the way across and then back again. You can keep going back over the nose three or four times if you wish to make a more three-dimensional nose.

When you are happy with the nose size and thickness, end the next stitch at the bottom middle of the nose. This is the point where you will make a line down from the nose to create the mouth. You are essentially making an upside-down Y shape. (See pages 59–60, Basic Bear, for more photos of this process.)

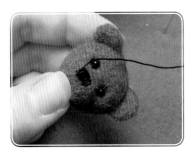

I like to lay the thread down to see where it will finish, making sure it is straight and ensuring I'm happy with the look. I find that the one-piece head also suits a smaller space between the nose and mouth.

Take your needle in at the bottom of the line above where the mouth will be. Your needle will go in at the middle and out on one side, then back in at the middle and out on the other side. Take the last stitch in at the middle again and then back out through the back of the head as shown.

EYEBROWS

Once your nose and mouth are done, the eyebrows are next. I find getting the placement of the brow can take a few attempts. Often I will get the first one perfect and the second one just won't cooperate, so be prepared to remove your needle, pull the thread out, and start again.

Before you begin you need to select your eyebrow style (see some examples in the diagram above). You can see the different expressions you can get from different brows.

Once you have chosen placement, bring the thread out at the top of one eyebrow, generally above the eye. Lay the thread down the side to give yourself an idea of how the eyebrow will look.

How close do you want the eyebrow to be to the eye bead? How long will it be? Each bear is different and you can try a few things. Don't anchor after the first brow or it will be hard to pull the thread out if you have to start again.

Take the stitch down near the eye, and then come out at the top, in an equal position to the top of the first brow. Come down again and make the stitch match that on the other side, bringing the needle out of the back of the head this time.

Check you are happy and then anchor off.

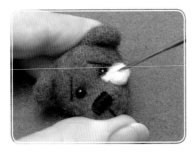

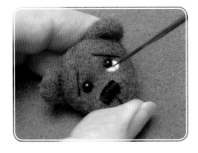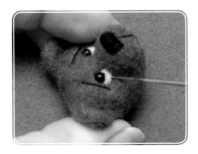

EYE WHITES

To make whites under the eye beads I prefer to use a fine merino fiber. It gives the best finish with no hairy fibers sticking out.

Taking just a few strands of fiber, make two small balls of wool. They will be roughly the size of half a pea.

Using the smaller needle, poke the whites slowly and not too deeply under the eye bead. Work carefully, making small pokes along the edge and under the bead.

Once you are happy with the position of the white, do the other eye white so that each is partially felted only and positioned as equally as possible.

Then finish felting both of the whites in place.

Eye whites take some practice and different placements give different looks. If you don't felt too deeply to start with you can always pull them off and start again if you are not happy with them.

MAKING THE BODY

The body is, again, the easiest part. Start by mixing the fiber and rolling into a loose ball.

Begin felting with your large needle or multi-needle tool, poking and turning to keep it round.

As it begins to firm up, roll the piece firmly between your palms, forming a fat sausage. Needle one end to a point and the other into a fat, round end.

You can manipulate the piece, as was done in earlier projects, by pinching the point and needling the fat end with inward pokes to fatten it up. Once the fibers start resisting the needle, change to your finer one and keep poking and turning to create a smooth, evenly shaped egg.

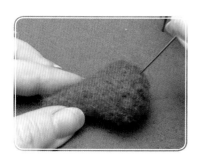

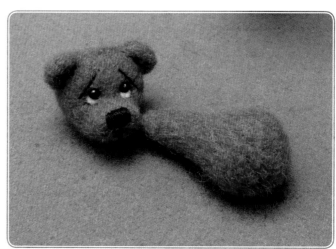

Jointing as you go or jointing at the end? Either way is fine, but there are pros and cons to both. I showed the latter approach with the basic bear — first creating the parts, then putting them together. You can see the whole bear this way, and plan where the pieces will go. I prefer to joint as I go. I can't lose any pieces this way, and I often find a bear begins to form its character as I work and so I may decide on the shape and style of each part as the bear comes together. You can choose to do what suits you best — it won't affect the final results. See pages 84–85 for the jointing photos for this bear, and pages 65–68 for the Basic Bear.

MAKING SCULPTED ARMS

Mix and split the fiber into two equal amounts. Roll each piece in your hands to get an idea of how big the arm will be. Adjust the amount of wool, removing and adding fiber as needed.

Begin by rolling each piece into a sausage shape. Then, holding the piece at the one end, start felting down the arm from the other end, poking and turning as you go.

The end you are holding will be the paw, so keep felting along the arm, coming in at the end as well as along the sides until it is fairly firm.

It pays to work both arms at the same time, so start the second one before beginning the paws. This way you can ensure they are the same size and shape.

! When making limbs you want them to be evenly proportioned. So for both the arms and the legs, work in pairs.

Making these arms requires a little more fiber than arms with just one bend and the limbs can seem a bit long until they are shaped. Remember that you can add more fiber to the paw end if you don't feel they are long enough.

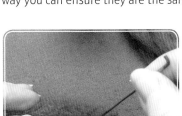

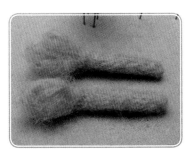

To begin the paw, work it almost into a ball shape, coming in at all angles to firm it up. Then flatten it, and keep turning over to firm it up.

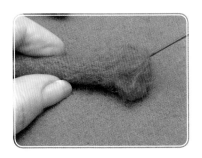

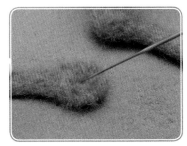

Work around the edges by holding the piece between your fingers. Just felt slowly, turning as you go. This should create a nice round paw. Your pieces will look like strange lollipops at this stage!

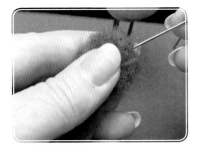

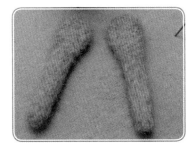

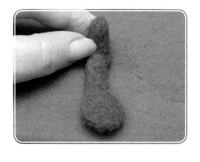

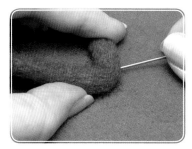

Now to put the bends in the arms. The placement of these bends makes all the difference to how the arms will look.

When your pieces are almost firm, put in your first bend. This will be an L shape just down from the shoulder end of the limb.

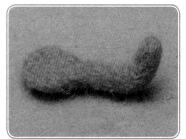

Remember to needle the bend from all directions to get it to hold well. (Note that this paw is turned inward, i.e., not the same way as the basic bear.)

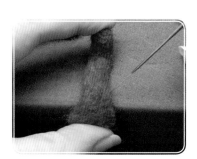

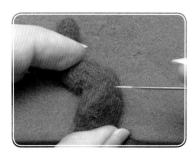

Do this bend on both arms and test how they look against your bear. As you hold the limb against the body, think about where the next bend for the paw will go. The plan is to have it going around the front of the body and dropping downward.

The wrist bend goes in now and then you can shape the limb around the body.

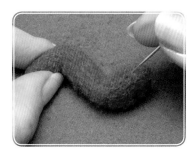

Holding the limb with the shoulder up, bend the paw down and felt into place. Again, be sure to felt from all angles to get the shape to hold. You will also want to shape the paw more, so work the entire area.

I will often joint the arms on at this stage so that I can get the best shape possible, but you can hold them if you are more comfortable doing it that way. The limb will curve around the belly and you can needle it against the body a little, just remember not to felt too deeply or for too long without moving the arm away or it will attach itself. If it is still a little soft, hold it in the desired shape and felt it on your foam until firm and smooth.

MAKING THE LEGS

Take one large amount of fiber and mix. Pull apart into two equal pieces, roll each into a ball and then firmly roll into a sausage. Compare sizes at this stage as you can add and remove fiber to match them up.

Begin working the limb from one end only. This helps to ensure both are of equal size as you can add and remove fiber as you go.

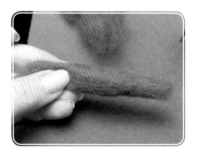

Start poking and turning the sausage, working down to just over half the length of the piece. To keep it nice and thick you can come in on the end, felting slowly and deeply into the length of the leg. Then go back to felting across the width. This helps to ensure the fiber is well felted in all directions.

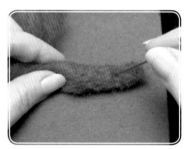

Change down to your finer needle, working until the leg feels nice and firm. Felt both legs to the same point to help keep them equally sized.

Now you can compare the loose ends and make sure the felted ends are the same length.

If happy with the amount of fiber you can move on to the next stage. If not, you can add and remove pinches of fiber at the loose end until they match.

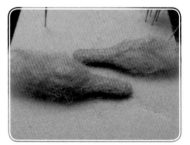

Using your larger needle begin felting the loose ends lightly all over so that they will compact and thicken up. It will begin to look a bit like a lollipop.

Remember the ends will appear a lot larger than you want the foot to be, but it will shrink when it is felted.

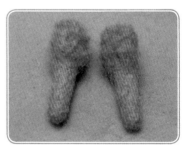

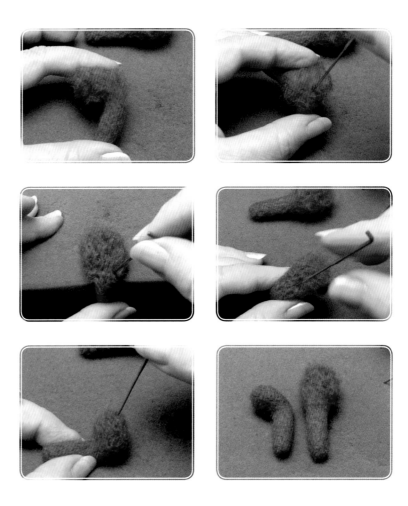

Fold the pre-felted foot over the leg and needle the heel area a number of times. Once it is holding, flip the leg over, putting the foot flat on the foam. Needle inwards from different directions to shrink the foot down.

Flip over and place the leg down the edge of the foam. Work the bottom of the foot to make it nice and flat.

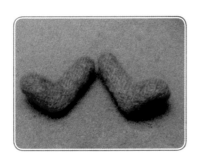

If the foot seems a little soft and flat all over you can pinch it gently between your fingers and work around the edge as you did for the ears.

Keep checking the feet together to try to get them as similar in size and shape as possible.

Once you are happy with the shape of the feet, change down to the finer needle and finish firming them up.

TOE PADS

To make toe pads you need six small pinches of fiber and two slightly larger ones.

Roll the balls two at a time between your fingers, one in each hand. This is to compare the sizes and is the easiest way to get them roughly the same.

Depending on the fiber, either roll into balls or felt lightly to hold the shape. Some fibers will hold well just from you rolling them in your fingers.

First place the heel pad and with the smaller needle work from the center outward to attach. Then neaten the edge by felting around it.

Getting both feet the same can be tricky, but it does help if you do the toe pads in the same order for each foot.

Next place the middle toe pad, and again using your smaller needle attach by working from the center outward.

Add the toe pads on either side. They can overlap slightly at this stage as they will shrink a little as they attach.

Remember to only partly work each piece so that you can still adjust once all are loosely attached.

Only when you are satisfied with the placement do you felt the edges to get them neat.

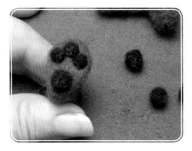

JOINTING

For more detailed written instructions on jointing your bear, please see pages 65 to 68, Basic Bear. As I mentioned at the beginning of this project, you can joint as you go or once all the parts of the bear are complete.

JOINING THE HEAD TO THE BODY

Poke the needle into the bottom of the head where the neck would be and take it out through the top. Pull the floss through leaving about 3 in (10 cm) hanging from the bottom of the head.

Now enter the top of the head in exactly the same place as the needle came out. Take the needle back through the head to come out next to the thread left at the neck.

Next, take the needle from the top of body and travel right down to the bottom, taking the needle right through the body and gently pulling the thread until the head and body are touching. Go back through again, exactly where you came out, and take the needle up to the neck next to the thread that's there. Pull the needle through and remove, leaving the floss.

Making a firm half knot you can turn the head to see if the head is sitting at the best angle. If you are happy with the placement of the head, keep the thread tight and finish the knot. Then flip the bear over and tie a second knot.

Remember, don't cut the threads yet. Thread them both back onto the needle and take the needle in between the head and neck joint. Enter the body and exit anywhere in that piece.

Holding the thread tightly, cut against the body so the floss will disappear back into it.

The head and body are now attached.

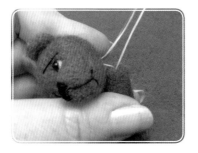

JOINING THE ARMS AND LEGS

With the basic bear, I joined the legs first. Here I joined the arms first. It really doesn't matter which order you prefer to do it in.

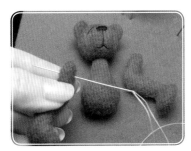

Take your needle, threaded with 12 in (30 cm) of floss and insert it on the inside of one arm and take it through and out the other side. Remember to leave a 3-in (10 cm) tail to tie at the end.

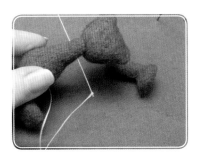

Then insert the needle next to the thread, making a small stitch, and come out next to the tail of thread that you left.

Take your needle in again at the matching point on the body where the arm will go. Take the needle right through, ensuring it is straight and level across the body. Pull the floss through so that the first arm is now touching the body.

Enter the second arm from the inside, coming through to the outside and taking a stitch as before. Take the needle into the body next to the other thread and come out the other side. Pull the thread through and remove your needle.

You now have both arms attached and the threads are next to each other ready for tying off. Finish in the usual manner and then do the same steps to attach the legs.

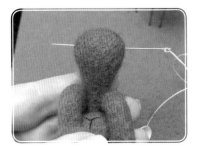

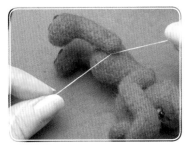

ADVANCED RABBIT

In this project you will learn more advanced styles and techniques which you can add to your bears and other critters. The most noticeable difference with this creation is the two-piece muzzle. This gives a really cheeky look which is cute on bears as well as rabbits. I will also show you how to make the lovely long rabbit ears and the cute belly blaze that really sets this bunny off.

Some of the instructions are for things you have already learned like jointing, making bodies, etc. Instructions for these may not be as in depth as in earlier projects so please check back to these if you forget any steps.

YOU WILL NEED:

- Fiber in main and complementary colors
- White fiber
- Beads for eyes, $1/8$ in (4 mm)
- Thread for bead attachment
- Sewing needle
- Felting needles, large and small
- Foam square

TO MAKE THE HEAD

Take a handful of the main color and mix the fibers together by pulling the wool apart and teasing it in different directions.

Now roll into a loose ball and using the larger of your felting needles or your multi-needle tool, begin to poke and turn the head.

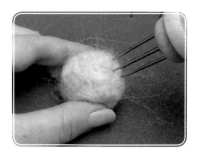 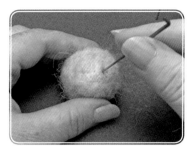 

You need to keep turning every four or five pokes to keep the piece round and to stop it from attaching to the foam. Keep poking and turning until fairly firm.

CHEEKS

You don't need very much fiber for the cheeks, but they need to be the same size. Mix the fiber as before and split into two equal parts. Roll these in your palm firmly to get an idea of their size. Add or remove fiber until you feel they are equal and then felt as before.

Felt until firm but not hard. If you are using a finer fiber, such as merino, you may find that with smaller amounts you need to change down to your finer needle to get it a little firmer. Remember not to make it so firm that it is too hard to attach.

To attach the cheeks to the head, hold them against the head as shown in the photo opposite and felt deeply a few times. Check their positioning and when you are happy, felt into and all around the cheeks so that they attach well to the head.

If you remember how the position of the muzzle in the Basic Bear project (page 55) was manipulated, that method can be useful here.

You need to squeeze and press the head up so that the cheeks will move down to the bottom of the head (as in the photo to the right).

When they are firmly attached you can change down to your smaller needle to help shrink them down a bit more and even out the surface. Then felt all over.

NOSE

Take a smaller amount of wool in your nose color and roll into a ball. Pre-felt this a little with the finer needle as the larger one won't work well on such a small amount of fiber.

Felt this ball directly onto the top join between the cheeks, plunging your needle in at all angles to get a good attachment. If the nose is a little small you can always add more fiber. If you feel it will be too big, though, it may be best to make another one and attach that instead.

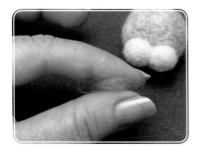
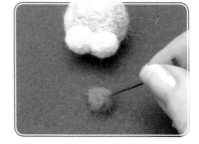

EYES

Make indentations for your eye beads by felting with your bigger needle in one place where you want the socket to be. You can enlarge the size to suit the bead by felting in a little circle until the socket is deep enough.

When both sockets are done, anchor your thread by bringing the needle and thread through the back of the head and out at the socket, then enter the socket again in the same place. This way you won't make any stitches that can be seen, and there are no knots either.

Pull firmly to be sure the thread is well anchored and then thread the bead and bring the needle from the socket to out at the back of the head.

Pull firmly again to ensure the bead sinks a small way into the head, then take the needle in from the back of the head and out of the other socket.

Repeat the process and anchor off by going back and forth through the head. Cut under tension so that the thread end disappears.

The fiber I'm using has a lot of flyaway hairs. So holding my small scissors against the head I trimmed off the surface to make it a bit less fluffy. I also needled around the eye beads with my fine needle to tame some of those fibers too.

EARS

To make the ears you need two equal amounts of the main color fiber. How much you use depends on how big you want your ears to be. You can make them any size. The main thing with these ears is not to make them too thick!

Felt a little fat sausage from your fiber, keeping one end unfelted.

Keep poking and turning until it just starts to firm up and then start felting it down flat. Flip over regularly so it doesn't stick to the foam.

Also hold it between your fingers and felt up and down the sides to make a nice smooth edge.

Keep the ears as even as you can by felting one ear and then measuring the second one against the first regularly as you go.

Once you are happy with the shape of the ears continue felting until they are smooth and firm. You won't be able to felt the ears once they are attached so make sure you are happy with the shape and how firm they are before you felt them on.

As with the bear's ears, remember to leave the bottom of the ear where it attaches to the head unfelted.

Now you can decide where you want to attach your ears.

 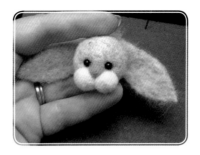 

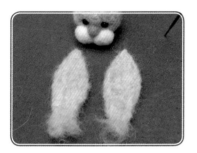

I've shown three possible placements in the photos above — upright, side of head and top of head. You can choose what you think makes your bunny look best.

Attach to the head by the unfelted ends.

Remember that you can tack the ears on with just a few pokes to make sure you are happy with placement before you attach them well.

Start with your larger needle and then move on to your finer one to tidy up when the attachment is complete!

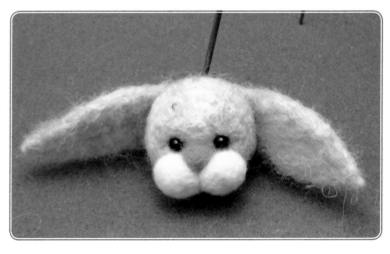

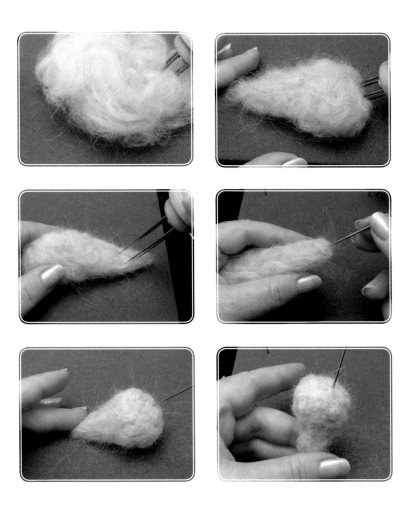

MAKING THE BODY

Take one amount of your main-colored fiber, mix, and begin felting a large ball.

As the ball begins to firm up you can start to pinch off one side to make more of an egg shape. Roll the ball in your hands to help create this shape also.

To make a nice plump bunny bottom felt the bottom of the egg shape directly and keep turning to keep it rounded. To make a longer, more elegant rabbit, keep the body longer.

Keep felting all over with your larger needle and change down to your finer one as your work starts to firm up.

Gauging quantity is probably the hardest thing to master with felting and you may find your first projects are often too large or too small in places, but you will get there!

ATTACHING THE HEAD

Attach the head to the body as usual. Remember to check the placement and find the front of the body after the head is attached as we want to do the belly blaze in the right place. If you try to do the belly before attaching the head it is very hard to get it in the right place!

BELLY BLAZE

Take a small piece of the white fiber (or whatever color you are using for your blaze) and mix it a little before felting on your foam.

As this is a flat patch that is attached directly to the belly, it is good to think about a few things before you begin.

First, the shape. You want a teardrop shape that matches the shape of the body and it needs to be the right size. Remember to make the patch a little big as it will shrink when attached. I find that for this shape I can felt it a little and then pull on the fiber to elongate it and get the thinner, more pointed shape that I want. For this smaller amount of fiber, use the finer needle and flip it over on your foam regularly so it doesn't attach itself.

Again, you can felt along the sides to help define the shape while holding the fiber between your fingers. (Warning: you do get a few more holes in your fingers doing this but it is totally worth it!)

Needle the piece straight onto the belly, working from the center outward as always. You can either work the edges and have a well-defined edge or let it be a little fluffy as long as it's well attached.

I tried to show in the photos that my blaze looks a little holey up against the body. To combat this, firmly rub your fingernail up and down the surface to fluff it up a little. Then continue felting with a fine needle. You can felt and rub over a few times to get the surface more even.

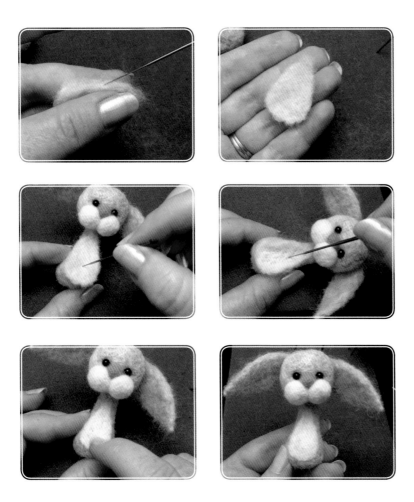

MAKING THE ARMS

I have kept the arms basic for this rabbit as there is enough going on with everything else to make this piece interesting and we don't want to hide the belly too much.

Take a handful of wool, mix and split it so you have two equal amounts. Roll each piece in your hands to get an idea of how big the limb will be. Adjust the amount of wool, removing and adding fiber as needed.

Holding the wool sausage at one end, felt down the limb, poking and turning as you go. The end you are holding will be the paw, so just keep felting along the arm, coming in at the end as well as along the sides until it is fairly firm.

It pays to work both arms before starting on the paws as this way you can ensure they are the same size and shape.

When you are ready to work on the paw, almost felt it like a ball, coming in at all angles to firm it up in a round shape. Then flatten it and keep turning over to firm it up.

Knowing when a piece is at the right firmness to begin shaping takes time and a lot of practice. You will make mistakes but don't get discouraged! Until you have over-felted a piece, making it too firm to shape, you won't know what too firm feels like. If it is too soft when you begin shaping, you can spend a long time shaping your piece while it keeps flattening out and changing shape on you. Remember to think of everything as lessons learned.

Work around the edges by holding the piece between your fingers. Just felt slowly, turning as you go.

This should create a nice round paw and, at this stage, your piece will look like a strange lollipop.

You can now add the bend to the arms.

Make an L-shaped bend in your limb, and holding it on the foam square, felt at all angles to hold the shape. Remember to flip over.

Once it is holding the shape fairly well, change down to the finer needle and begin firming up the piece.

It's up to you what angle your paws are on, but you can hold the limb against the body to get a better idea of the shape you want.

Work all over until firm and smooth and ready to attach.

ATTACHING THE ARMS

Attach as usual (see page 85).

MAKING THE LEGS

Begin as for the arms, though using perhaps a little more fiber. Work down the length of the leg until you are happy with its length and it is fairly firm.

Next felt the loose part which you have been holding (the foot) until it is a soft ball. You can tell if both feet will be the same size at this point so add or remove fiber as needed, bearing in mind that you want nice long bunny feet. Needle the fiber until you have a soft ball on the end of the legs.

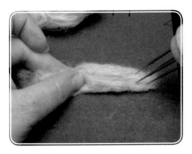

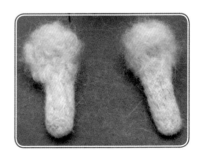

Fold this ball over the leg, so that you are looking at the bottom of the foot. Make some deep pokes with your larger needle to form the heel. Now flip back over and work the top of the foot from all angles, keeping it plump and not allowing it to flatten.

Work around the edge of the foot to make a smooth side from the heel to the toe. Remember you want a longer foot and it's OK if it is a bit flat. Keep working until firm and then change down to the finer needle. You can add toe pads at this point if you wish (see page 100).

If you need more instructions for making or attaching these parts refer back to earlier projects, especially the Basic Bear.

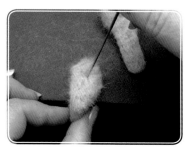
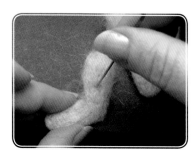

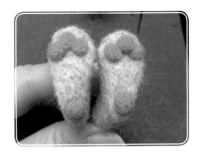

TOE PADS

For each foot I took six pinches of fiber and rolled them in my fingers, checking for size. Then I used two slightly larger amounts for the heel pads. These can be felted straight on after a little felting on your foam. Work slowly, though, keeping the edges tidy and watching the placement of the pads.

I like to add the heel pad first, then the middle pad at the top. This way the end result is likely to be similar for both feet. However, it is quite hard to get the pads in exactly the same place on both sides. Keep in mind that usually only you will notice any little differences like these. Anyone you give your bunny to will think your work is amazing. Don't be hard on yourself for not having things exactly the same.

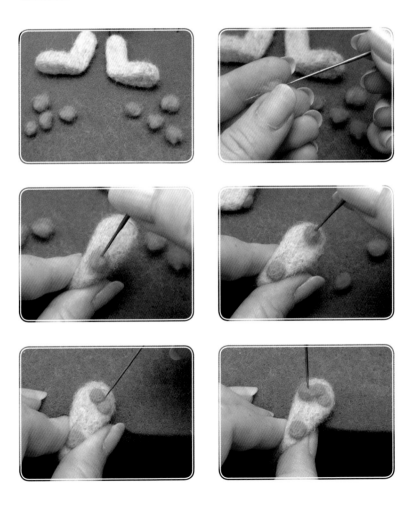

ATTACHING THE LEGS

This is done the same way as the arms. Remember to check placement before you tie the final knot and keep all the pieces pulled tight so that your jointing will be firm.

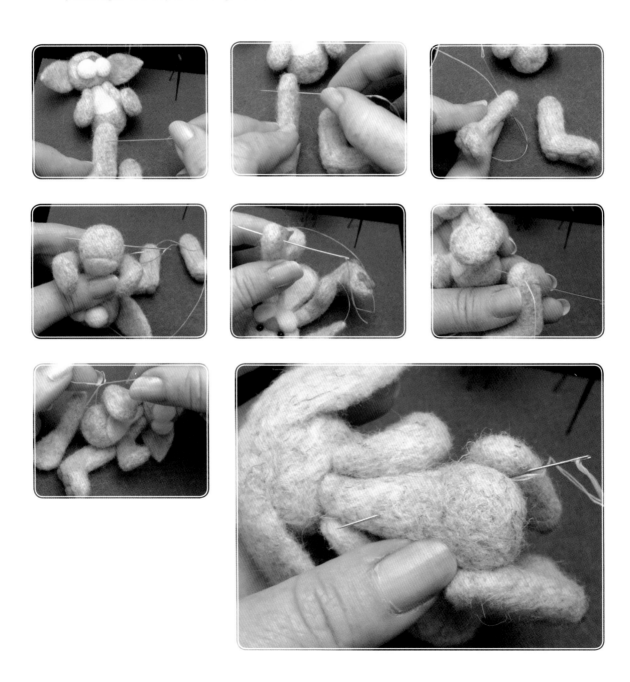

BUNNY TAIL

Nearly finished!

Don't forget to give your bunny a tail. This is just a small amount of fiber worked into a ball and attached to your rabbit's bottom while it is still only half felted.

I like to keep the tail fuzzy so I haven't worked it for too long. Just enough to be sure it is attached well.

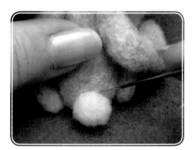

I am sure you now have a wonderful bunny creation to be proud of! As I said at the start, this two-piece style of muzzle/cheeks can be used on other critters. So have fun trying it out.

Other Rabbits

I wanted to show you a few different styles of rabbit. Some are made with one-piece heads and there are different shapes, sizes and placements of ears.

You can add little things like teeth or change how the ears sit on the head to give each rabbit its own unique style.

I've made the teeth shown above right by adding a pre-felted piece of white fiber at the Y section of the sewn mouth. I have then taken a stitch in black thread right down the middle to create the gap between the teeth.

Accessories, variety and color will keep your work interesting. There are more ideas on the following pages.

MAKING YOUR BEARS (AND OTHER CRITTERS) UNIQUE

ACCESSORIES

Now that you've made your lovely felted bear it feels like he or she needs a little something else. Maybe you are thinking just a bow, or maybe a little pendant or a hat? Sometimes it is hard to think of the perfect accessory, but it is easier if you collect little things that might be suitable whenever you come across them. I have miniature cakes, scooters, beds, chairs, etc. and pendants and necklaces in containers. I like using ribbons on my bears, so I have a huge boxful in lots of colors so that I am sure to find something that works with my bear.

You can make lots of things, too, such as wire glasses (look online for instructions) or wings. Headbands are cute and easy for little girl bears, and certainly help to make them look more girly — which is tricky with bears sometimes. A bit of gathered fabric or lace makes for a gorgeous little skirt.

Collars, if kept small, can give your creation a vintage feel, or a big collar creates a clown! Run a thread along a narrow strip of fabric and pull it in until it is the right size for your bear's neck and tie it on.

If you can knit or crochet you are lucky (and one step ahead of me!). I can't do either very well but have produced a few hats and scarves for my critters. You can see in the photos opposite that I've made some sewn ones too.

While it can be tempting, try not to over accessorize your bear. Choose one or two things, or keep it simple with just a bow.

EYES

They say the eyes are the window to the soul, and that seems to be the case even with felted bears! I get many comments about how much character my bears have in their little faces and I put it down mostly to the eyes.

Earlier in the book I described how to add white under the eye bead (page 77) and this definitely gives the bear more soul.

You can add other colors at the eye socket too. The little blue bear holding the button (top left) has a darker color added in above the eye bead.

The little pastel bear (middle left) has larger eye beads. This gives a wide-eyed baby look. It is amazing the difference less than $1/16$ of an inch (1 mm) can make, but at the size you are making your critters tiny fractions of an inch between bead sizes can give very different looks. Note the much smaller beads used for the eyes in the bear bottom left.

You can also see the felted eyes option below. These are always big and expressive.

Where you put the eye bead matters too. You can see from these photos that some are right against the muzzle and some are a bit further away.

In the diagram I've shown eyes wide apart and slightly below the top of the muzzle, eyes closer together and up against the muzzle and eyes placed in the middle of the face. There are many variations on these looks and mostly placement is just experimentation and preference. If you look at where the eyes are on just about any bear or other handmade animal you will find more variation than you would expect.

MUZZLES

First, noses and muzzles are not the same thing. The nose is the bit at the end of the muzzle (stitched in the photos top and bottom right, but it also can be felted). The muzzle is essentially the entire piece you have added to the front of the head. Sometimes the muzzle is not a separate piece, but part of a sculpted one-piece head.

You can make your muzzles different shapes and sizes to give different looks to your creations. Sometimes the tiniest of muzzles can give a very cute look to a creation. Remember to do tiny stitches for the nose on a tiny muzzle.

If you are doing a two-piece head, your muzzle can be oval, round, squarish, or slightly triangular. If making a one-piece head, you might taper your muzzle down to a point or it can be almost non-existent. With all these options you can see how unique each of your creations can really be.

In the diagram on the next page I've shown you an oval muzzle, a triangular muzzle and a very small, round muzzle. Each picture has roughly the same shape ears and eyes at the same placement, so you can see how making a different muzzle shape can give a new look to your creations.

You'll also notice that for the wide muzzle I've done a wide nose, a triangular nose for the triangle muzzle and a tiny nose for the very small, round muzzle. But try any combination that you like.

NOSES

Noses can be stitched or felted, or they can even be clay pieces that you glue on. Most of my noses are stitched, but for variety I do felt some of them.

Most sewn noses are either a rectangle, soft rectangle or more of a triangular shape for smaller bears. As we have covered already, make sure you layer up your stitched noses so that they have a thickness to them as this will give them a better shape.

I also like to use mixed colors in my noses, often taking my colors from the fiber I've just made the bear from. You can also create a random effect over the nose with different stitching and colored thread. I like this almost messy finish for some bears.

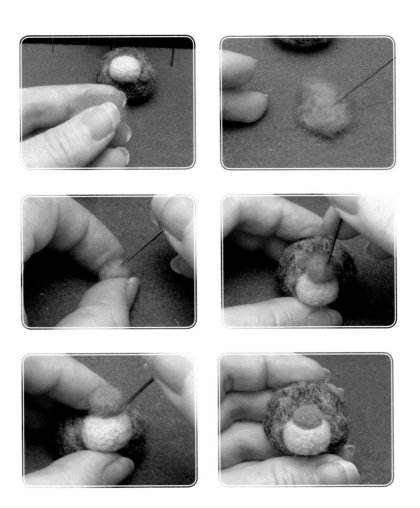

FELTED NOSES

Felt noses are simple (see the photos above), but sometimes attaching them can be a little tricky.

Make sure your muzzle is nice and firm, otherwise when you add the nose it will end up sinking into the top of the muzzle and look more like a belly button in the wrong place than a nose!

You can make noses any size you like, just remember to try it out on the head before you attach it. Because they are so quick and easy you could even make up a few noses and see what looks best.

EAR PLACEMENT AND SIZES

There isn't a lot of variety when it comes to the shapes and sizes you can make ears, but when you team up a size, color and position you can achieve something quite special to that bear.

You can see from these pictures that we have big ears, small ears, ears that are up and some that are down. Down ears can give your critter a really sad or babyish look. Slightly higher up and he looks a bit more of a charmer. Right on top, he's your typical little bear. You can see that bigger ears can give an instant mouse look, and I've had a few bears that have turned into mice over the years!

The method for any of these ears is the same, just remember to check your placement before you start felting and to only felt a little at the start so you can remove them if you change your mind.

One thing you might like to do is get a second color onto your ears. It is quite difficult. Often people will try and add another color to the front of the ear but it will go right through and the size and shape of the color added can change dramatically after attaching. When I want to add another color I use watercolor pencils or artist pastels. You can use the pencils just slightly dampened and rub them directly onto the ear or wherever you want it. If it gets anywhere else you can just trim it off. Build up the color, just doing a little first to make sure it looks ok. I like to add little cheeks to my girl bears in the same way!

BELLIES AND BELLY BUTTONS

Adding a plump little tum gives your bear a very cuddly look. You want to add these after all the limbs are jointed on so that you get the placement right.

Mix your fiber and prefelt a ball, then flatten it into the shape you want: it may be oval or round, that's up to you. How fat it turns out will depend on how much you felt it into a ball before flattening it. Remember to attach by working from the middle outward. These bellies look great with little dent belly buttons too.

Adding a belly button can certainly give an extra "cute" factor to your creation. I love to put them on very plump, baby-style bears but they will work on anything. We have covered just making the little dent in the projects, but you can also felt shapes on the belly, such as a tiny heart. If you can embroider you can stitch something onto a belly, or even a foot and it will look amazing.

I have added gemstones and other little things to bellies. All you need to do is felt a flat area to match the item you are going to put there, then glue it on with jewelry-strength glue. Remember to keep checking and felting until the gem will be a little recessed into the felt and no edges will show. Also, don't use too much glue. For felted shapes, pre-felt them on your foam a little first and just work slowly with shallow pokes to attach and keep the shape.

MAKING INTERESTING FEET

You've mastered the basics and now you want to make your bears' feet a little more exciting. The feet I make are all the results of experimentation; things I've tried out and liked. There are many that I tried and don't make anymore, too, but it's always worth making something new just to see how amazing it might be.

You can see that even just using different colors gives a great effect, but I also try different shapes, including my favorite two-piece pads (see instructions on page 114). This style of foot can be harder than it looks and getting the proportions right is important to a good finish.

Also pictured are single pads. A single pad is very simple but it can be difficult to get a good match between feet when you work with very small amounts of fiber.

You can add claws to the feet. In the photographs you can see they have all been added in different ways. Some are stitched through the pad and some are in front of it. You can add gems, embroidery, painting, anything you like to embellish your feet. Often artists will put their trademark on the foot, too, so perhaps you will come up with something unique to yourself that you will put on all of your work.

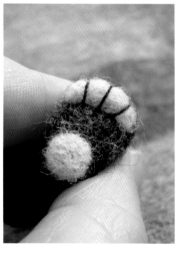

MAKING TWO-PIECE FOOT PADS

First, mix your colors and make balls for both feet. One will be for the heel and the other for the toes. Roughly the same amount of wool should work, or slightly more for the toes.

Needle the heel pads, then attach them.

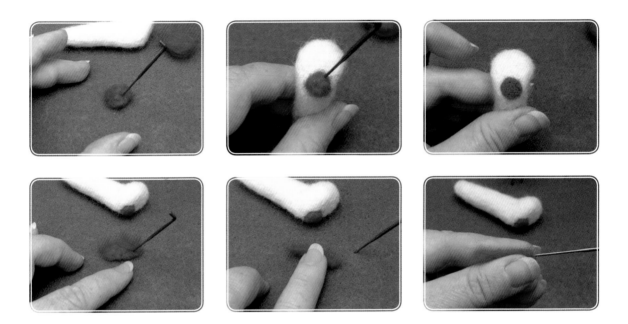

Then needle the other piece of fiber for a while before rolling it in your fingers to create a small length a little longer than the width of the foot. You can felt in from the ends to make sure it's nice and plump.

Holding it so that it curves around the end in the shape of the foot, needle along the edge.

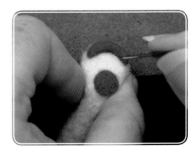

Then taking the needle into the ends do a few pokes to secure each end. Now you can felt the entire length all over. If it gets too flat just felt along the long sides again. Once attached you can do the sewing to create the claws.

Anchor off your thread and take it out at the top of the roll. Bring the needle down and into the bottom of the roll directly below the exit point above. Repeat this for as many lines as you want to have, then anchor off.

It can be tricky to get both feet the same. Remember you can always pull the fiber off or do the sewing again if you want to get them more alike.

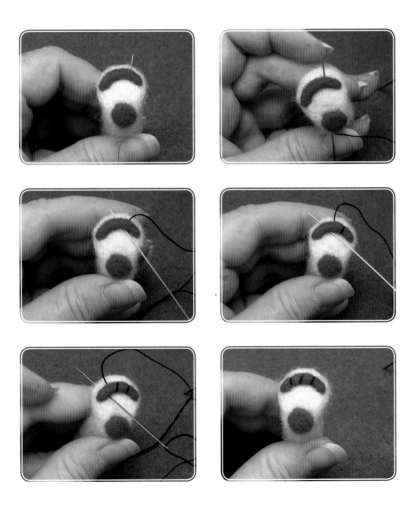

COLOR COMBINATIONS

Obviously you can felt with any colors you wish and you may have noticed that my work is always very colorful. I rarely work with just brown wool, although it can be easier to source. If you don't want to dye your own fiber, adding colored accessories or other things can keep it interesting.

I've been surprised over the years at what colors will work together well. I only really started using unusual combinations at the request of my customers. I remember making my first lime and purple bear and thinking it looked awful until I finished, and then I could see it was a great color combo.

Now I grab bags of wool and try the colors next to each other, making up combinations of two, three or even four colors that I want to use.

I also know of people who only work with white fiber and then airbrush colors and patterns onto it for exceptionally stunning pieces. Experiment and see what mediums you can use along with needle felting to create your unique style.

MAKING PATCHES

Although these instructions are for making a patch, you can apply them to any shape you want to add to your bear.

Add patches and other patterns after the bears are put together. Otherwise, you might spend hours getting something just right, only to have it covered by a limb or end up being at the back.

Felt the mixed-up fiber on your mat a few times with the finer needle. Flip back and forth and then needle flat the sides by pinching it between your fingers. You should only need to go around once or twice.

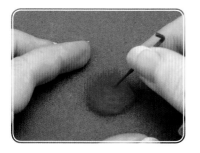 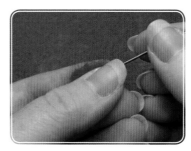 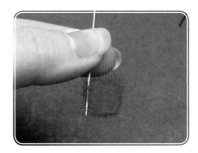

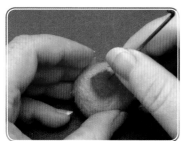 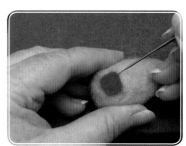 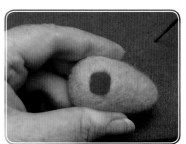

Attach in place and needle from the center outward. Then focus on the edges to get them even. You could leave it there and so not need this next part but I like to do this finishing with my patches.

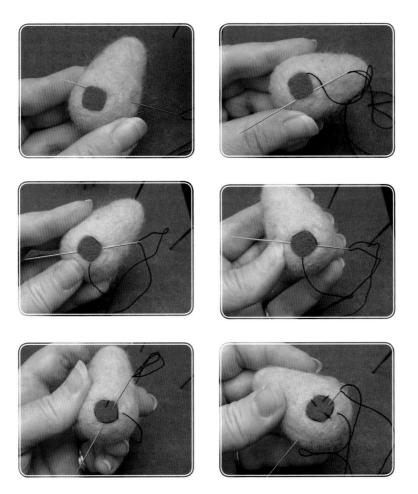

Using your embroidery cotton, anchor off the thread and then stitch long lines around the patch going from corner to corner. It doesn't matter what order you do them in, just as long as each side gets done.

Then, coming out at a point along one of the sides, you will take small stitches into the patch to give it that sewn-on look. Do this for a few of the sides. I generally don't do every side. It looks more random that way. Then anchor off and you're done!

MAKING FAIRIES

There are a few ways you can turn your bear or other critter into a fairy. Often I will just make a normal bear and decide after he's all done that he would actually make a fabulous fairy, and that's when he gets his wings.

Some people like to make their own wings using mediums such as clays and glass-like substances to achieve truly stunning fantasy pieces. I tend to keep it more simple and use wire or bought wings with nylon over them for color.

These are glued onto the back of the bear, but make sure you check the placement first. The bear needs to be able to sit with the wings on.

If you are making your own wings with wire, you can leave pointed ends free and then insert them straight into the bear's back. All you need to do is create a hole by needling in and out very deeply, almost like making a belly button. The trick is to get the angles and placement perfect. Then glue and insert.

This is also the way that I add antennae to my fairy's little head. I needle deeply, dip the wire in glue, and then insert into the hole I have made.

Adding other little details can really make your fairy special. Sometimes beading, glitter, flowers, etc. give the perfect finish. Just remember not to go too far; less is always more!

CREATING OTHER ANIMALS

By working through the ideas in this section you will see how easy it is to use what you have learned about making bears to create any critter you like. By making pointed ears (see page 122) and tails (see page 125) you can create cats and dogs. You can even make mice by adding a pointed muzzle.

Take ideas from here and use them to build your own set of skills. Always keep thinking, "What if I do it this way?"

In my next book I plan to cover making elephants and other animals as there are more techniques you can use to achieve excellent hooved critters.

MAKING POINTED EARS

Mix the fiber and split into two equal parts. Begin felting and turning as a ball until it is holding the shape and then flatten, turning frequently. When the piece begins to firm up, pinch it between your fingers so that you can create two sides for the ear. Work along one side, then flip over and do the other one. Remember to leave the wide end unfelted for attaching.

Measure them against each other to get them the same size. Felt until quite firm as you won't be working on them after attaching.

Check placement and ensure you are happy with where they are sitting before deeply felting across the back of each ear. Finish off with your finer needle to get a smooth finish.

MAKING LONG TAILS

You can use long tails for lots of critters. Making them is simple but it does take time.

Mix an amount of fiber and roll into a long piece. It doesn't matter how big you make it at this stage as you can always remove fiber from the loose end if it's too long. Keep it fairly thin, though, as a thicker tail doesn't look as nice.

Work up and down the length of the fiber, turning regularly as it will adhere to the foam quickly.

After you have worked up and down a number of times, pick up the tail and roll it in your hands.

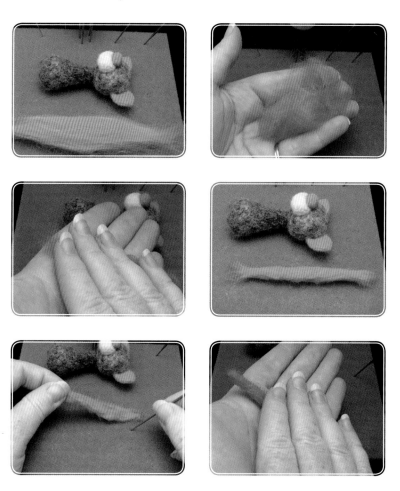

Now work in from the tip of the tail to give it a nice rounded end. You will probably find you need to change down to the finer needle by this stage depending on your fiber.

The tail will get a bit smaller after being attached, but felt it fairly firmly before you do so.

I like that these tails can hold a bend, so after it is attached you can manipulate it into a shape.

If you want a specific shape, before you attach it, you can put bends in the tail just as you can do with arms and feet. Hold it in the shape you want and then needle all around the bends.

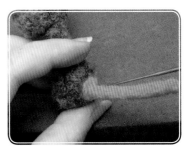

I've taken my needle into the loose fiber at the base and down the tail with a few pokes to bring in stray fibers and to ensure the tail isn't thin at the body end.

Now you can attach it to the bottom of your creation. I usually add tails last so that I am sure it is in the perfect spot. In the photographs here I did it before the legs were attached so you can see the process more clearly.

Felt deeply all around the base of the tail with your bigger needle and then change to the finer one to finish up.

Needle felting is an evolving craft — it can be anything you want it to be. Try new things, enjoy yourself and don't be discouraged when things don't work out. I have a basket of bear parts from my first couple of years; projects that didn't work out or limbs I had to do over.

I really appreciate your taking the time to work through my book, or even if you are just flipping through the pages, thanks for your interest. After ten years of needle felting I can honestly say that this is an amazing craft and if you decide to embark on this creative journey I'm sure you won't regret it.

You can always find me online if you need any help. I love talking with customers and crafters alike. Keep an eye out for my second book as there will be more great projects to test your skills and broaden your felting repertoire. And thanks again for spending time with me!

Liza Adams

Little Handfuls
MINI BEARS

ABOUT THE AUTHOR

My name is Liza, and I'm a mother of three who became addicted to needle felting almost ten years ago. I live in Hamilton, New Zealand, and have for most of my life. My husband is a computer addict (which is lucky as that is also his job). I put up with his computer quirks and he puts up with my addiction to small furry animals (real ones), of which we have quite a few in our home, including cats, dogs, guinea pigs and rabbits. The most exotic pets are a pair of Chinchillas. These little rodents are the fun in our evenings, which is when they wake up and start dashing about their cage.

My craft area shares the lounge with my husband, children and pets. This area has evolved over the years to almost take up half the room, much to hubby's dismay! But I just couldn't work shut away in another room. I need to be with the rest of the family, even if it means writing in the evenings. I do most of my work at night and I can't watch a movie without some project in my hands as well!

In 2004 a student in my parchment craft class showed me what she had been making at home — needle-felted bears. They were lovely, and piqued my interest, so the next time I was at a craft show I bought a kit. After making up my first creation, I bought a book and was then firmly on track to a woolly addiction.

When I first started out I used to do lots of online searches, looking for bears of all descriptions, trying out different paw shapes, muzzle sizes, and ear positions. Anything I could find a picture of I would copy onto one of the hundreds of pages that I accumulated for ideas and inspiration.

I tried never to copy another crafter's work completely. I would just pick a part of the bear that I liked and mix it with other styles to see how it turned out. Most of these first bears were given away but I do still have the very first bear I ever made (see right), and a few other early ones too.

I feel it's very important to find our own style as artists. You need to find your own niche and create your own style. The wonderful thing with needle-felted bears, as opposed to sewn ones, is that there are no patterns. No one else is using the same pattern as you and turning out the same bear over and over again. Needle-felted works are truly one of a kind, whether you are making bears, dogs, cats or monsters. Embrace that and go wild! People will love your passion as it always shows in the finished work.

My first bear.

Zachary

Austin

MY FAVORITE CREATIONS

I've made a few bears over the years that have been hard to part with. Some I made for orders and I hated sending them away. Some I made for myself only to have a customer fall in love and I just couldn't say no. I've learned to keep some as "not for sale" for a little while, so that I can enjoy them before they have to go. People often ask how I can give away such lovely little creations, and the honest answer is, sometimes I can't! But knowing that they are going to awesome new homes really helps. All my customers are wonderful.

Zachary would be one of my first favorites and he was the Little Handfuls mascot for my first ten years (recently retired). The new mascot, or face, of Little Handfuls is Austin.

Both of these bears include some of my favorite features —big feet, large bellies, and soulful faces. Zachary has a long knitted hat and Austin has lovely refined features and dropped paws.

WHERE TO FROM HERE

So far in my ten years needle felting, I have had a number of milestones. I've taught night classes, started a facebook page, traveled around the country to teach lovely ladies and their friends, and attended more shows than I can count. I've been on television for a craft segment which has been aired a number of times. I've won awards for my work, written for magazines in New Zealand and overseas, and been featured on many websites. I've sold my work in boutique gift stores, sent bears all around the world and received emails from people who love what I do.

Ten years ago I wouldn't have thought any of this was likely to happen, so I suppose that the next ten years could be filled with as many exciting things as the last ten. I have written my first book and am hoping to travel overseas and visit some international bear shows. I am working on my second book. This one has been a lot of work, but also a lot of fun. I hope you enjoy working through my book and thank you so much for your support.